ESCAPING CHRISTIANITY

~

FINDING CHRIST

Barbara Symons

Copyright

To Lyle:

My greatest ally,
my truest friend,
my biggest fan.
You are the standard bearer of truth,
loyalty and unconditional love.
There is none like you.

Contents

Notes to the Reader

Much of the information in *Escaping Christianity* came to me intuitively. As I wrote, I sought to relay the message as fluidly as possible with consistency in the terms used, however, I use Divine, Source, Spirit and God interchangeably. I do this because I feel the word "God" has too much religious baggage attached to it and I seek to free the reader from such limitation.

I also seek to present the Bible as highly symbolic, metaphoric and allegorical. This does not mean that I do not see its historical and literal value. While I present a version of scripture as metaphor, the reader is encouraged to find his or her own understanding.

In quoting scriptural references I have used a wide variety of versions. Each scripture was chosen with the intent of bringing the greatest level of understanding to the message I seek to share.

Those who call themselves Christians, but are not fundamentalists, may ask why I titled the book *Escaping Christianity*? The title reflects my personal exodus from a controlling and manipulative religious system. Escaping is what it felt like.

To clarify, imagine for a moment that you take a vacation to Los Angeles and find yourself in a crime-ridden part of the city. While visiting, you are mugged and beaten, even held temporarily captive, by fear. You write a book about your experience and call it, *Escaping Los Angeles*. The book does not imply that all of Los Angeles was like the crime-ridden part in which you found yourself, but nevertheless, your experience still happened in Los Angeles.

I use the word "consciousness" a lot. Surprisingly, many within the Christian culture misunderstand this term as it has a "New Age" connotation and as such is avoided. Miriam-Webster says this:

Consciousness *is the normal state of being awake and able to understand what is happening around you: a person's mind and thoughts.*

Also used are the words metaphor, allegory and template.

Metaphor *is a word or phrase for one thing that is used to refer to another thing in order to show or suggest that they are similar: an object, activity, or idea that is used as a symbol of something else.*

Allegory *is a story in which the characters and events are symbols that stand for ideas about human life or for a political or historical situation.*

A **Template** *technically speaking is a shaped piece of metal, wood, card, plastic, or other material used as a pattern for processes such as painting, cutting out, shaping, or drilling.*

For the purposes of this book, a template is what helps us see another pattern emerge when a mystical interpretation is set upon a literal example.

Escaping Christianity ~ Finding Christ is about my journey out of Christianity and my return to critical thinking. It brings into focus the sector of Christianity called fundamentalism that believes in the literal and rigid interpretation of the Bible and that embraces doctrines and dogma (unquestioned beliefs) that endorse control, intolerance, division and judgment. There are millions of souls who have been hurt and even damaged by this system. It is to those individuals within this system, who have been held captive spiritually and emotionally, that I seek to bring light and understanding.

But it is so much more than that. I hope to shed new light on the symbolism that may be found within the Bible's metaphoric and allegorical teachings. So much of what Jesus taught is not reflected in mainstream Christianity. I left the Christian church system and I no longer call myself a Christian, as it is defined today, but I do wholeheartedly embrace the teachings of Jesus Christ found in the Bible and other mystical texts. I no longer believe what someone else tells me to think. I discern for myself.

I also use the names and terms Jesus, Jesus Christ and Christ a lot. Jesus is the name of a human and Christ is a title bestowed upon an awakened human. As you read you will come to understand the application of the name and title.

Absent from this book are the doctrines that enslave the minds through controlling religious systems. If you would like a fresh perspective on an ancient character and teachings, then this book is for you. No matter what your faith or your absence of it, you will find this book enlightening and thought-provoking

Preface

Your work is not to drag the world kicking and screaming into a new awareness. Your job is to simply do your work ~ sacredly ~ secretly ~ and silently ~ and those with "eyes to see and ears to hear" will respond. The Arcturians

The book you hold in your hands is my work. It is the result of forty plus years spent within Christian fundamentalism. During those four decades I was an active participant in what I came to realize was elective brainwashing—a process I willingly subjected myself to because I wanted and needed to be right with God. I had to be part of a system of belief that I felt had the market cornered on truth, and especially on heaven. It may sound harsh to describe my experience as brainwashing, but it has been a lengthy process of deprogramming, spanning the last fourteen years, that allows me to justify this definition. The brainwashing began when I was just five years old, too young to know better, by continually subjecting me to fear-based theology, not only from church leaders, but members as well. Generally speaking, Christian fundamentalists employ behavioral modification techniques of separating themselves from anyone who does not share their beliefs or specifically follow their dogma within a particular sect. I learned to judge and separate myself from everyone and every system of belief that did not coincide with my fundamentalist beliefs. I looked down upon those who strayed outside the perimeters of my dogma. I continually looked for and needed consensus to feel safe. As I grew older my worldview narrowed to the point that it seemed everyone else was in danger of going to hell, but my cronies and me.

As a child, I had visions of hell, torment and eternal separation from God. I just knew that the rapture would happen and I would in some way fall short and be left behind. I believed in a God who hated certain people and that I could be one of them if I did not believe in what I was told and behave in an acceptable manner. I believed that God killed his son as a sacrifice for my filthy heart. If I believed in Jesus and accepted him into my heart, that same God would spare me from hell where people were tormented night and day, night and day, in eternal flames of torture amongst rotting, stinking flesh. Belief in Jesus was supposed to be my "get out of hell free" card. But it seemed that according to fundamentalism, even that wasn't good enough. I needed to behave my way into heaven by obtaining the approval of those around me. There is something called *pastoral covering* in fundamentalism where a church member must submit themselves to the pastor and or his leadership team. They are the spiritual behavior monitors within the system that determine whether one is sinning or not or behaving in a manner that puts them in jeopardy of right standing.

I recently spoke with a friend, who like me, has been transitioning out of fundamentalism for over a decade. We realize now that we were profoundly damaged by the system. To think outside the fundamentalist box is considered anathema; a term that means to be damned or dedicated to evil. I have been told that I am deceived, of the devil, a witch and a Satanist. I have suffered the loss of many friends because I see things differently than they do. I have been the subject of sermons, and have been mostly disenfranchised from the church in my small and conservative city. However, with the help of retrospect, I am deeply thankful for every difficult and painful experience, for they have brought me to where I am today— free.

I speak with many transitioning Christians who in good conscience cannot exist within the limiting, dogmatic belief systems. What ultimately happens is, as they begin their exodus, like me, they want their friends to see the insidiousness of their programming and try to dismantle the system from the inside out. Unfortunately, that just doesn't work and it's also not the pattern set by Jesus when he had conflict with the religious systems of his day. They forced him out of the synagogues and temples—so he taught in the fields, in homes, gardens, boats and mountainsides. Structured Christian fundamentalism cannot contain the ever-expanding consciousness of its namesake, Christ. These religious systems built egocentric institutions that, in order to survive, must pander to the human ego.

Ego-dominant structures will always be threatened by such freedom, for in that freedom there is no consensus, and where there is no consensus there is fear. The ego needs to be, and must be, right.

Our freedom lies within our ability to shed the restriction that keeps our consciousness from unfolding, like the "old wineskin" that Jesus taught about. Covered in more detail later, the old wineskin is a metaphor for an old way of thinking and perceiving reality. This old way of thinking cannot contain the new consciousness of the kingdom age that Jesus spoke of. Jesus demonstrated the pattern for freedom that clearly defines how to shed the restrictiveness of fear and notably fear-based religious systems or the *Law* (Old Testament behavioral patterns).

It is my hope that the information within this book will in some way help to awaken those seekers still enveloped within fundamentalism, and display the unconditional love and hope that this Savior of theirs so eloquently expressed through the holistic and metaphoric interpretation of his parables. I know of many spiritual seekers within Christianity who will not speak of their evolving beliefs or their doubt concerning some of the more absurd doctrines within the church fearing that if they do, they will suffer the loss of relationships and standing within their church community.

Those within the grasp of dogma who have been subjected to years of programming will feel a good measure of discomfort as they read this material. The discomfort they feel is a key indicator of their level of indoctrination. I encourage them to press through. They may read for curiosity's sake, but even then they will receive the seed sown in love for humanity's collective slumber and will someday receive a gentle nudge to awaken. The seed of Christ has been sown in each human being and that seed, when confronted with the water of unconditional love and non-judgment cannot help but grow. Numerous parables hint at this truth.

I spoke at a conference in October of 2010 where a woman sitting in the front row, pulled the microphone out of my hands and began to gently rebuke and renounce my message eluding to Christianity's limited interpretation of scripture. In April of 2012, she attended another conference where I was speaking. Again she sat in the front row and this time when I finished speaking she grabbed the microphone and shouted,

"*I get it! It took me a while, but I am awakening!!!*"

This woman is in her late 70's, which just goes to show you that it is never too late to bloom.

I hope to share with the spiritual seeker the phases that I passed through as I exited fundamentalism:

- Deprogramming
- Shifting Consciousness
- Understanding the (scriptural) Templates
- Embracing Your Divinity

This book is a handbook of sorts to help those brave pioneers as they begin to navigate into the "age to come" as Jesus put it. The migration out of dogma and literalism will provide a footpath from perceiving God externally to embracing the Divine within. This process is aptly called "inversion" and helps to identify the Christ nature intrinsic in all. It is where we see that the stories in the Bible and other spiritual texts should be considered archetypical rather than historical. These stories are told down through the ages to remind humanity that we are, collectively, the subjects of the myths. We are the Son that was given, we are *the Christ*. With an inverted lens, the stories have not occurred outside of us but rather they reveal our internal, spiritual and Divine development. *Christ in you, the hope of glory.*

In the movie, *The Notebook*, the character, Noah, reads to his wife, Allie, from a notebook filled with memories of the life they shared. Years earlier when Allie was diagnosed with Alzheimer's disease, she recorded the events of their life together in the notebook and told him to read it to her when she forgets who she is. And she remembers.

That's us!

We have forgotten who we are. Humanity is speckled with cultural stories and myths that serve to awaken us, to remind us of our origin. However, in the case of fear-based Christianity, fear keeps us focused externally telling us stories of hell and separation unless we believe in its version of the truth. It is simply not so. This Bible is here to remind you of who you are. It is one of many books that tell us; remind us, of our story.

I attended a Writer's Workshop where we were given an exercise. We were to complete the following phrase:

I used to be _____ *but now I am* _____.

As I stood up at the microphone in front of the workshop audience, I made the following declaration:

"I used to be a fundamentalist Christian and now I AM."

Judging from the eruption of applause from the audience I know that this book is timely, even for those who may never have been involved in fundamentalism but are eagerly awaiting the awakening of people just like me.

If you have been involved in new age, metaphysical, self-help or popular psychology you will be inspired by the hope that is imparted through this book and it will also issue a challenge. I spoke recently at a Unitarian Universalist church in my hometown and voiced this simple truth,

"Those that are most tolerant are least tolerant of those that are intolerant."

I have found that some Universalists are radically and wonderfully inclusionary except when it comes to those that preach intolerance. There is a measure of distain within some inclusionary religions for fundamentalist Christians. Christianity has earned its intolerable reputation but we must not throw the baby out with the bathwater lest we be the same as fundamentalists. Non-Christians have a skewed view of the Bible because of those that thump it. It is to our benefit to learn and appreciate the rich metaphorical and allegorical language within it; in particular the teachings of Jesus. Most will find appreciation of scripture if it is introduced as metaphor, unconditional love and acceptance rather than from an historical, literal, exclusionary, and intolerant view. They will understand that the Bible is a guide to man's journey in consciousness, and what a beautiful story it is.

Now, onto the book—I hope you will savor every word as I have while doing "my work."

Phase One

Deprogramming

Chapter One

The Deer in the Hog Trap

If I can escape, anyone can. By "escape", I mean to exit the mindsets that define fundamentalist Christianity. Deprogramming was paramount in my spiritual journey out of religion and into Christ consciousness, forsaking the history for the mystery. During the late 1990's, my awareness began to shift and I started to see linear biblical events as internal and mystical rather than external and historical. As such, the stories within the Bible provided me with a wealth of metaphorical information, like a treasure map to my/our personal and collective evolution in consciousness. Along with this mystical view, of course, came a lot of rejection from my church brothers and sisters. However, something was overtaking my old system of belief and there was no turning back. I was seeking and I was finding. It is my desire to share this journey so that it may help activate what I know is already latent within you.

In his book, *UnThink: Rediscover your Creative Genius,* author Erik Wahl states,

> *"Often the only time a boss or company will see the need for change is when the change has been made without permission."*

This seed of change in consciousness is already within you and it is germinating without your permission. Consciousness is evolving rapidly and long held beliefs and prejudices are crumbling as the forerunners break the way into new thought. What an exciting time to be alive. Those that pander to fear and fear-based systems of belief will be the dinosaurs as we see the *age to come* emerge.

I want to stimulate your intuitive sense and nudge your awareness to perceive a broader purpose for life here on Earth. Wahl beautifully describes our intuitive function when he says,

"Intellect without intuition is a smart person without impact. Intuition without intellect is a spontaneous person without progress."

In the *age to come* it will be vital to develop our intuitive function. Our consciousness has largely been suppressed by intellectualism and our intuitive abilities bound with fear. For those who have never been restrained by literalist fundamentalism, you will likewise benefit from this material. Who has not been stifled by some sort of fear? Whether in relationships, the workplace or religion, it is time to lose the shackles. In this age it is all about increasing awareness and breaking free from all intuitive restriction. In my case, Christ consciousness could not be restrained in a limited fundamentalist environment. The root that was Christ within me had broken out of the pot. Humanity is poised for the single greatest leap in our conscious evolutionary ladder if we are brave enough to lay aside the beliefs that no longer serve us and exit the structures of fear that have so restricted our expansion.

Recently, I introduced metaphorical interpretation of scriptures to a friend still within fundamentalism. In a period of twenty-four hours, I was called brainless, mindless, deceived and the devil. If you threaten the pulse of a fundamentalist, be prepared for a backlash. Questioning literalism is akin to treason within this Christian camp.

Firstly let me say that the Bible is not a Christian book. Anyone who knows the history of the Bible knows this to be true. Generally speaking it has been hijacked by the Christian religion and further by fundamentalists who have interpreted it with lenses that promote literalist dogma rather than truth. Intuitive functioning has little place within fundamentalism. Conversely, this book takes a deep dive into the symbolic language of metaphor found within scripture and will stimulate the underused intuitive part of our brain. It is through embracing the mystical messages found in the Bible that we begin to see the patterns and templates emerge that, among other things, awaken us to see our underlying identity as Divinity. We will see through the mystery of the parables and other scripture that Divinity, having no material form, planned a willful descent into our material plane to find for itself a helpmate (the human body) from which to explore, create and inhabit physical worlds.

I recently read this:

"I think, therefore I am no longer a Christian."

This is a sad indictment indeed. For those outside the walls of fundamentalism it is not hard to see that within it, reason has given way to a systematic and dogmatic approach to knowing God based on fear. So polarized and schismatic are the teachings within some sects of fundamentalism that they only associate with others who agree with them. I have had several friends within Christianity that, by their choice, are no longer my friends. They have severed ties having been threatened by my evolving views.

People leaving fundamentalism are making the return to critical thinking and discerning enough that their minds may open to information outside of dogma. This message is also for those who desire to understand these mysterious scriptural texts without becoming a slave to religious structures that corral the mind with fear. Let's put the spotlight on the scriptures themselves so that they may speak loudly and clearly when they are seen through the lens of mystery rather than history. Viewing the scriptures mystically opens the door wide to all people. You don't have to be a Christian, a Jew, or claim any religion. You can be an atheist and yet still find commonality and confluence with the metaphorical interpretation of the Bible.

I no longer call myself a Christian, but I am a follower and a believer in the teachings of Jesus.

Furthermore, to embrace the teachings of Jesus Christ is not to become a Christian.

Christianity has given themselves (and Jesus) one horrendous black eye and I can certainly understand the reticence of non-Christians to embrace the Bible. However, I feel that now more than ever before, a great awakening is upon us and with this awakening comes a greater ability in consciousness to interpret these metaphorical mysteries. Presently, like the story of Jesus sleeping in the belly of the boat *(Mark 4:39)*, Divinity slumbers within, while mankind dallies in fear and fear-based religious systems, as the frequency of fear is incompatible with the love of Divinity. In the pattern and example displayed in the life of Jesus, never once was he driven by fear, and neither should we. When we leave fear behind it becomes possible to lay all judgment aside, to really love one another, and embrace the truth of who we are and why we are here.

The advent of the life and teachings of Jesus were like a bomb dropped in the Bible. So diametrically opposed are most of his teachings to the rest of the Bible that we fail to bridge the gap in understanding that fact. He came to rescue those held hostage within the grasp of religion by introducing love, non-judgment and tolerance. He fulfilled all of the requirements of the *law* when he expressed unconditional love. This is to be our journey in consciousness as well. We are to "follow" Christ.

Jesus actually manifested the next age outside of time itself. He spoke often of the *age to come* because he embodied it. He plopped down, smack dab into a religious society that was holding the hearts and minds of men captive through ritualized religion and fear. He came to set men free from such tyranny. The bomb dropped was consciousness clearly evolved past the environment it found itself within; it was in fact from another time, another age, even another dimension.

I no longer call myself a Christian, but I am a follower and a believer in the teachings of Jesus. I also recognize that the term Christianity is a brand defined by limited consciousness within religious antiquity, which now at best only represents a shadow of the message of Jesus Christ. Generally speaking, today's Christianity might be a parallel comparison to the Judaic religious system that Jesus opposed. During that time it is recorded that Jesus was continually hard on the pious for their rigid adherence to a system that was being dragged past its season of relevance, and for their reticence to let go of it.

People will remain within restraint as long as they need to; although a pearl is formed in one, the process is ongoing in another.

Ultimately, the mysterious things he spoke of and taught through the parables and his apparent abandonment of their laws, threatened them.

The religious folk just did not get it. Might that religious system be a mirror of the fundamentalist system today—intolerant, judgmental, full of fear and threatened when followers do not adhere to their dogmatic traditions? This is a common theme throughout our human history. Is this not the basis for most conflict in our world?

If we take a holistic and historic view of scripture, Jesus wasn't a Christian as is defined today. Moreover, he wasn't even a good Jew. Jesus modeled a way for us out of systematic, ritualistic and fear-based religion. If we are to grasp his message metaphorically, he was hard on the archetypical Pharisee, that is, the egocentric drive within all men that flourishes within fear-based systems. Metaphorically, the Jewish nation is allegoric for an ego-driven consciousness that manifests in all of us while Divinity struggles to reveal itself under continual threat of annihilation. Scripture tells of Divinity's chronologic journey into humanity using this group of people to physically express the fundamentals of humanity and its journey in consciousness. To help awaken fear-bound consciousness, Jesus came to them, to stimulate their intuitive faculties by using rich, symbolic language that must bypass the intellectual ego, like a thief in the night to reveal latent Divinity, the pearl of great price, hidden within man. It is said, *"Behold I come as a thief" (Revelation 16:15)*

Metaphor is a thief that gently robs us of our literalism while we transition into the intuited worlds that wait anxiously for our *conscious habitation.*

In fundamentalism, through repetitive programming, I was made to focus on fear and literalism. Not unlike most fundamentalists, I became more of an archetypical Pharisee, loving rules and rituals rather than loving people. My egocentric self needed to be right rather than righteous. I rejected symbolism because it messed with my dogma. These are hard statements for Christians to swallow indeed. I know it was for me. Coming out was a harrowing process and spanned years of heartache and confusion. I was fighting for the return of my critical judgment as I waded through decades of piled high, dogmatic poo.

But as hard as it was for me to understand this, I see now that religious systems are, for some, absolutely necessary. Human consciousness evolves both individually and collectively and for some, religious structures are beneficial while their individual and growing consciousness are in need of rules, regulations and boundaries. For a time, we are cocooned within our limitation undergoing intrinsic changes in our consciousness and in our physiology.

This fledgling consciousness is like a child in need of parental guidance. The scripture speaks of this in the book of Galatians:

What I am saying is that as long as an heir is a child, he is no different from a slave, although he owns the whole estate. The heir is subject to guardians and trustees until the time set by his father. So also, when we were underage, we were in slavery under the elemental spiritual forces of the world. But when the set time had fully come, God sent his Son, born of a woman, born under the law, to redeem those under the law, that we might receive adoption to son ship. (Galatians 4:1-5)

There is a need for all of us to experience restriction until Christ is formed within—like a pearl within an oyster, closed tightly until the time of harvesting. Before I understood this principle, I tried to convince others to leave the system as I did and in retrospect, it was before their time. I felt like a cage fighter; only my opponent was the cage itself. I was battered and beaten by trying to dismantle the religious system from the inside out as I tried to liberate those still within its grasp. I now understand that people will remain within restraint as long as they need to. Although a pearl is formed in one, the process is ongoing in another. My problem was that I was still programmed to proselytize. Oftentimes I experienced a life lesson that helped me understand this process, like this one:

Texas has a rather large feral hog population and occasionally they "camp" for a few days near our home and cause a lot of damage tearing up the lawn as they look for their favorite meal of grub worms. I have read that hogs can smell them up to eighteen inches below the surface of the ground and their tusks can easily overturn the rugged Texas turf to find them. Feral hogs are notoriously migratory in the open country and so my husband, Lyle, sets our hog trap each time we see evidence of them returning and rooting around the property near our home.

Not long ago, Lyle set the trap with corn, a meal that hogs love. Unfortunately, deer and other wild animals love corn meal too. He usually mixes a small amount of diesel fuel in with the corn so that the other animals will not be drawn within the cage and become trapped inside. Feral hogs, it seems, don't mind the sweet smell and taste of diesel and eat the corn anyway. This time however, he forgot to include the fuel. We woke up the next morning hearing strange yelps from the pasture and looked out to see a beautiful buck trapped inside the hog pen. Harry, our Great Dane, was beside himself wanting to go out to investigate the latest game in the pokey. We had to restrain the one hundred and eighty five pound Harry inside the house while we went out to free the buck.

As we approached the cage, the buck was flailing around wildly trying to escape and causing a great deal of harm to himself. We stopped moving toward him hoping he would calm down but it became evident that we just needed to get the cage opened as quickly as possible and set him free. Lyle had difficulty getting hold of the gate because the buck was ramming his head and snaring his rack in the top of the cage, moving it several inches each time he struck. His rack stood over a foot above his head and any way he turned he would tangle within the steel grid and hurt himself. The trap is less than four feet high and the buck struggled to stand within it. He charged the cage again and again and again.

We opened the door but the buck was too scared, too hurt, and too wild. Lyle, while holding the spring loaded gate open, told me to go to the opposite side of the pen hoping that the buck, being afraid of me, would turn away, see the open gate and leave. However, the most amazing thing happened; as I arrived at the other end of the cage the buck stopped his violent movements and stood perfectly still, watching me intently. He was bleeding badly from his nose and air was bubbling out through the bloody and torn sinus cartilage just below his left eye. I bent over slowly to look at him. His head and rack lowered to match my gaze. There we were, standing less than 18 inches apart, eye-to-eye; still.

I was overcome with compassion and a lump formed in my throat. This beautiful creature stood before me badly damaged and battered. With our eyes locked I blinked away tears and said softly,

> *"I am so sorry, poor thing...I am so sorry. You are okay...be still. You're okay. You need to put your head down, turn around and leave...the door is open. Put your head down, turn around and leave, the door is open. You are free beautiful boy, you are free."*

His eyes did not leave mine and he watched me ever so carefully. I slowly lowered my eyes to the ground. I swallowed hard seeing his self-inflicted wounds bleeding profusely and making a puddle onto the grass below. In the wee hours of the morning, still and quiet, I could hear the patting of the blood as it hit the ground.

A minute or so had passed and my back ached from bending over. I moved ever so slightly to straighten and suddenly the buck put his head down and with a swooping motion he turned around and exited the cage running swiftly toward the open pasture, his beautiful white tail disappearing in the brush.

Lyle and I walked inside, utterly amazed at what had just happened. We sat at the kitchen table sipping our coffee when suddenly I realized that this battered and wild animal was a reflection of me. Looking into the eyes of the deer and telling him to be still and that he was okay, felt now like I had been speaking to myself. After numerous painful experiences within the church system where I had the emotional stuffing knocked out of me, I saw me—beaten and battered by my own doing, fighting and resisting the system instead of leaving it completely behind. *"Put your head down, turn around and walk out of the door."* Those were words for me and for anyone who has tried to pull circumstances past their season of relevance. Finally after years of battling the dogmatic fundamentalist systems and the subsequent relationships formed within them, I have put my head down, turned around and walked out the open door.

I saw me—beaten and battered by my own doing, fighting and resisting the system instead of leaving it completely behind.

Everything changed when I left fundamentalism; my worldview, what I saw as truth, and my understanding of who we are and why we are here. I was filled with wonder at the increasing and holistic view I was beginning to see. It was like I had climbed this big hill overlooking a beautiful view and I was peering out through the parting trees at something magnificent. Our story is broad and vast and the implications of such truth will severely threaten the prevailing religious systems. For those spiritual seekers outside of these religious structures inversion is necessary. We must begin to see our cultural mythologies not as external and historical events but rather as glimpses into our internal spiritual construct and its principles, aiding us in our awakening, our evolutionary processes and ultimate reconciliation of our purpose here on planet Earth. You have planned and charted your course to be here at this moment in time—and you are right on time.

Summary Points:

- Bible interpretation: History or mystery? Literalism or mysticism?
- The Bible is not a Christian book.
- To embrace the teachings of Jesus Christ is not the same as becoming a Christian.
- Fundamentalism is fear-based and as such is incompatible with the love that Jesus spoke of.
- Jesus was not the founder of the system of Christianity.

- Jesus was not a Christian as it is defined today. He was not even a good Jew.
- Human consciousness is continually evolving and it is blossoming past restrictive religious systems.
- You are free. Put your head down (humble yourself), turn around (repent or change the way that you think) and walk out the door (leave restrictive fear-based systems behind).
- Fundamentalists will reject you when you challenge them or if you leave the system. Leave them alone. People will remain within restraint as long as they need to.
- The events recorded in the Bible are actually glimpses into ourselves, revealing our journey and our evolutionary processes in consciousness.
- You must overcome fear.

Chapter Two

Left Behind—Fear-based Theology

I was five years old when we got the news that our neighbor's infant daughter, Jane, had cancer. She was only a baby and had a very swollen tummy. The doctors ran many tests and ended up doing exploratory surgery that revealed she had cancerous tumors almost everywhere in her little body. Back then, her mom, Anna, (my Mom's best friend) had been given fertility drugs to help her to get pregnant. Jane was about two years old and dying. In a moment of extreme despair her parents experienced an angelic visitation; Jane experienced a miraculous healing that night—after struggling for nearly eighteen months, Jane's cancer disappeared. Her case was written up in the medical journals. This was during the Faith Movement back in the 1960's and was my family's initial immersion into charismatic Christian fundamentalism.

When miracles happen, they tend to validate whatever structure or belief system they occur within. In this case, the God within fundamentalism was, to Jane's family and mine, the God who had healed her. In my young mind, I thought everything in fundamentalism must be true because *that* God healed Jane. Now, I see that the faithfulness of Divinity works even while our consciousness slumbers beneath the blanket of the ego and within corrupt fear-based systems. Divinity does not judge us. It does not judge the systems of belief we find ourselves within. It just loves us.

When I was six years old, I also experienced an encounter with something otherworldly. A white light appeared in my bedroom. I remember it like it was yesterday. Lying in my bed, I no longer saw walls within my room. I was, it seemed, in outer space. A pinpoint of light appeared in the upper right quadrant of my view—so penetrating was this light that it hurt and caused me to squint my eyes. It, or I, moved closer and as the distance between us narrowed, the brilliance was stupefying. My heart bumped wildly within my little chest as this star-like beam pressed into me, seemingly to penetrate my right temple as I felt an odd pressure-like sensation there. After a few moments I didn't think I could take it anymore although, I didn't know what "it" was. I was not afraid but I was overcome. As the weightiness of this event lifted, I actually felt the compressed springs in my bed release and I lay there bouncing up and down, up and down and then stillness. I opened my eyes to see the sunlight coming in through the curtains and I clutched my little stuffed dog to my chest. Then from my belly came a thrust upward and out of my mouth came an unfamiliar language.

I ran into my parents' room still feeling the gush from my belly—speaking words and phrases unknown to us. "Tongues!" they told me excitedly. I had been given the gift of tongues. I was never shy as a child, so I got dressed and ran outside to tell my friends and neighbors—well, to tell and to demonstrate to anyone that would listen, about this unusual ability.

As a youngster, I attended many charismatic Christian fundamentalist meetings and other various Christian services—twice weekly home churches, my Lutheran church and numerous retreats and conferences. I knew all about heaven, hell, the devil and Jesus. I knew how to get people saved so that they would not go to hell. I was well informed about the rapture and those who would be left behind if they did not embrace the same message as me, spending eternity in torture and flames.

During some meetings I would be apprehended by a palpable presence and I would feel electricity wafting over my body. I felt at times as though I was walking through a highly charged energy field, especially when I walked into a room where people were gathered, praying or worshipping God. It was a wonderful addiction—I could not stand to be outside of this presence. However, fear began to build as hell and the devil were continually spoken of and soon eclipsed the joy that I felt in those meetings. It became imperative through threats of separation and condemnation that I speak their gospel message and try to convert as many over into Christianity as I could. It must be right I thought, after all, this God healed Jane. I bought into this religious system because of the fear that had been mingled with the miraculous. As a youngster I thought that if I didn't believe like the rest I could die and be left behind. Little did I know that this form of control, specifically the threat of hell, is a form of child abuse. I have heard it said that it is "ideological blackmail."

At age fifteen I wandered away from it all and took up with a faster crowd at school. When my dad passed away suddenly, I decided that I should get back to "God." The only way I knew how to get back into his good graces was through the fundamentalist church, so down the rabbit hole I went.

At nineteen years of age I had been attending a non-denominational fundamentalist church in Milwaukee, Wisconsin. I had recently broken off a three-year relationship with my boyfriend when the Pastor called me into his office for a meeting. He told me that I needed to rekindle my relationship with this young man and that God had told him that we would eventually marry. I wondered why God wouldn't tell me the same thing? I had respect for this Pastor but I was confused at the level of control that he was trying to enforce. I did not do as he suggested, and I stopped attending his church. The following year I married Lyle, my childhood sweetheart and husband now of 36 years. A couple of years later, I was further disillusioned to hear that the Pastor left the church abruptly with several thousand dollars from the building fund and the church secretary. After that, I would pop in and out of many churches over the next couple of decades before settling into a charismatic Methodist Church in 1991. Here I found my niche as a teacher, lay counselor, administrative elder, and deliverance minister (sort of like an exorcist). Lyle, our three boys and I attended faithfully, barely missing a Sunday for almost nine years. I held hundreds of deliverance sessions and saw many, many miracles.

The beginning of my deprogramming happened rather suddenly. One day my friend, Felicia, and I were chatting about a mutual friend that was very sick and in the hospital. Worried about her eternal salvation Felicia asked,

"Do you think Sarah is saved?"

I went to reply and suddenly my mind went completely and totally blank.

"Saved?" I questioned.

Felicia replied, *"Yes, do you think she is saved?"*

I felt my heart begin to beat a little faster and a warm flush come over my face.

Again I said, *"Saved?"*

Felicia, now a little agitated said,

"Yes, do you think she is saved?"

I shook my head, thinking maybe I was having a stroke or some kind of neurological event because I truly did not know what that word meant. Looking down at some age spots on my arm I grabbed a chunk of skin with a pinch lifting it upward and said,

"Am I saved?"

I was amazed at the wrinkles that I saw and the feeling of being "mortal". Somewhere deep inside I knew I was not "saved". Some other awareness was seeping through my consciousness, an awareness that had been percolating within me for months.

"What's wrong with you?" Felicia asked. *"Of course you are saved"* she said.

My mind was still blank. It was reminiscent of my first computer, a 386 HP crashing and returning to the DOS prompt, flashing white numbers and letters on a deep blue screen. It was gone. "Saved" was gone. I could not for the life of me remember what the word meant according to my Christian programming and dogma. I had been delivered a knockout punch like a boxer in a ring. Pow!

This single "aha moment" catapulted me into a different understanding of this exclusionary and divisive Christian doctrine. Somehow I had experienced an involuntary shift in consciousness— new understanding exploded within me. I had recently been searching, questioning a lot of doctrine, rethinking my ministry and was extremely dissatisfied. A few months earlier, I can remember holding a meeting in my home when, through many tears, I told of this growing dissatisfaction, pounding fists upon my knees saying,

"There has got to be more than this!" Soon after that meeting, I became fascinated with the subject of immortality. Could the word "saved" mean that we don't die? That day I looked down at my aging skin and clearly saw my mortality and knew I was not "saved". The Bible mentions the concept of saving the body but fundamentalism has relegated this precious truth into something exclusive, dogmatic and trite. The word "saved" means not to perish and I saw people, Christians, all around me, perishing. A big part of my deprogramming process was simply to question what it means to be "saved." Losing the word turned my world upside down. It was the first domino that fell and that started me questioning other critical tenets of my faith that no longer made sense.

In 1999, I ceased to belong to any church. My journey out of Christian fundamentalism has spanned more than a decade with many tears, triumphs and tragedy. I had, for my whole adult life, willingly submitted to fear-based church systems that spoke continually of eternal damnation, separation and hell. It was then that I started to see that I had repeatedly subjected myself to mind programming and brainwashing by religious leaders and more importantly to subtle behavioral modification by other Christians. I had also done the same thing to others who I saw backsliding or in rebellion. It seemed normal to withhold affection, acceptance, validation and sometimes, even friendship. How very sad.

I remembered a friend back in high school who had joined the "Moonies." At the time I thought, how could she be so gullible? Her parents traveled across the country to find her and subsequently spent a lot of time and money on counseling and deprogramming processes. I chuckle now because much in the same way, I am the one going through deprogramming.

This departure from mainstream Christianity was sudden and dramatic and a little scary. For years following I considered myself a recovering charismatic Christian, having had a spiritual breakdown/breakthrough/breakout of fundamentalism. I was apprehended by something larger than my religious concept of a Christian God. I began to see that the God of the Old Testament was a reflection of our own dual nature, a God that loved and hated, rewarded and punished, gave life and took life. And to some degree we needed such a reflection, a God we could relate to in our dual and immature state of consciousness. But Jesus told us of his Father, the Creator that is not punitive, but loves us and desires us to be one (consciously) with Him. My dogmatic palaces had no choice but to crumble under the weight of such love. I saw for the first time that the God of the Old Testament was not the same as the Father that Jesus spoke of in the New Testament. The Bible presents three stages of our conscious evolution. To understand this, it is critical to see it as a mystery book, so much more than a history book.

These three levels of consciousness are:

The Old Testament represents humans as egocentric beings in need of governance for their corrupt consciousness (old consciousness). We see God externally and through the eyes of fear and fear-based processes. It's all about following rules and regulations and is based on dualism—the knowledge of good and evil. This consciousness is left-brained logic based in dualism.

The New Testament represents an introduction into transitioning consciousness that is exiting the law and fear-based systems. During this transition we still need systems of behavior to guide the blossoming consciousness that would one day be fully embraced. Jesus demonstrated and manifested this new creation and what they would eventually become...if they believed.

Very truly I tell you, whoever believes in me will do the works I have been doing, and they will do even greater things than these. (John 14:12)

Paul was given guardianship over human consciousness during the transition out from fear as the fledging seed of Christ grows within the construct of the mortal human being.

My little children, of whom I travail in birth again until Christ be formed in you. (Galatians 4:19)

This migration is out from left-brained egocentric dominance and into right-brained intuitive function. It is also migrating out of dualism. The appearance of Jesus within the New Testament offers a radical view of one who was in no way subject to fear and the knowledge of good and evil. This consciousness has been reunited with his Father.

Fear works well to restrict consciousness.

The Book of Revelation is a detailed account of this transition, culminating in the overcoming of egocentric consciousness—awakened to love and entering the age to come. This book travels through consciousness and vividly explains, through rich metaphoric content, our unfolding as participants in the perilous and cataclysmic drama that forms the Christ within.

Birth is not easy. The narrow way we travel in consciousness, forsaking the former egocentric mode of being is like dying; a process that is necessary if we are to enter into the age to come.

Now, outside the system, rejected by my peers and deeply disillusioned, metaphorical understanding of scripture was overtaking my formerly held literal views. Being ostracized propelled me to write about what I was beginning to see. Departing the institutional church helped shift my awareness greatly out from literalism into mysticism as I was no longer subject to fear. However, there was a lot pain from being rejected and from being disenfranchised. I spent many, many days in deep despair. As my mystical vocabulary and understanding increased, more and more of my Christian friends left, believing that I had been deceived and was in danger of losing my salvation. Recently a very close friend of twenty-two years told me that she no longer wanted to be my friend because we were just too different in the things that we believed. I told her that if commonality in our spiritual beliefs was a prerequisite for friendship then we were in trouble.

Although these experiences have been painful, they have helped me to understand the depth of programming that has taken place within Christianity and other fundamentalist religions and systems. People within these systems are in need of spiritual healing. We have all been, at some level, held captive by fear, whether it be a person in an abusive relationship, in the workplace or a member of a religion, fear works well to restrict consciousness.

19

A year after we resigned our membership, I was hired by a local company where the owner had close ties to my former church. After I was hired, my immediate supervisor told me that if I was ever to hold any spiritual meetings at my home, particularly if other employees were invited, that the owner of the company would have to approve of the speaker and content in advance. When I questioned this she told me that the owner felt that he was an apostle of sorts or shepherd over his employees and that he was only trying to "guard his sheep." Finding it a little hard to believe, I took the matter to the owner and politely asked if it was true; did I need to ask his permission to hold meetings in my home? He enthusiastically said, "Yes."

Even outside of the church system I felt a measure of control over my actions. It seemed that fundamentalism reached deep into the local culture and psyche in our small town. The more I withdrew from church, the more I no longer fit in my conservative city. As I began to overcome some of the fear in my personal and professional life that had shaped my character and consciousness, I no longer felt the need to submit to controlling people and systems. I was not afraid of being perceived as *unsaved*, *backslidden* or *lost*. For the first time in my life I had a real sense of spiritual freedom. Momentum was building within me that fueled my confidence as I learned about Divinity outside of the church system. I was like a bloodhound, locked onto a scent and I was relentless and fearless as I progressed, like a person blind from birth—I could suddenly see. My dogmatic dominoes began to fall en masse; each one gathering inertia tipping over the next and the next.

As time moved on, aggravation, frustration and grief accompanied me many days as manipulation and control appeared woven in and through the fabric of my consciousness. Struggling to keep my head above the water, I felt the grasp of fundamentalism taking a swipe at me many times, trying to take me down into the depths of fear. Then conversely, deep regret for the many unrecoverable decades given to fundamentalism fueled my unraveling as I sought to distance myself from everything fundamentalist. It seemed I was throwing the baby out with the bath water, even barely able to pick up a Bible for years. I desperately needed a new set of spiritual lenses. Hearing any dogma was like dragging fingernails on a chalkboard. Flipping through channels on my television I would cringe at the sight of any televangelist. I simply could not stand to hear one more gut wrenching plea to get someone saved or to solicit money. I wondered how I had not seen this manipulation before?

Many tear-filled altar calls are made to get people to raise their hand, walk the aisle and to say the *sinner's prayer*. Fundamentalism says that accepting Jesus into your heart in this way means that you will be spared torment in hell when you pass from this life. They would say, *"Will you be spending eternity in the arms of Jesus or in the eternal flames of hell?"* This is their idea of salvation, as it was mine for decades. This concept of accepting Jesus into your heart is actually not in the Bible however it has morphed into standard fundamentalist doctrine over the last century. I was recently chatting with a woman that is a member of the United Pentecostal Church who questioned me concerning this very thing. She asked,

> *"Do you still believe that we have to accept Jesus into our heart to be saved?"*

I replied with, *"Did you know that is not in the Bible?"*

Then came a protracted pause....she looked at me and I could tell she was searching her mind. *"Yes it is",* she replied firmly.

I asked her to find the verse for me so that we could chat further about it sometime. Needless to say she has not found it and won't because it isn't there. A lot of liberty has been taken with the scriptures to create most fear-based dogma and doctrine. The command to "fear not" or "be of good courage" appears hundreds of times in the Bible so it is interesting that Christian fundamentalism is a religious system largely based on fear. The fear of hell, the fear of torment, the fear of separation, the fear of loss—fear is a great motivator and fundamentalism uses it well.

Challenging fear-based systems will be paid at great personal cost. But in order to really know the love Jesus spoke of, we must overcome fear. There is no way around it. Christian fundamentalists are hard-wired with fear and it will take a lot of conscious effort to re-wire their thinking. I know it did for me.

Down through the ages fundamentalists have created many controlling doctrines to support their system of religion, building upon limited revelation and acquiring consciousness constructed with fear. Being saved has nothing to do with raising a hand, reciting a prayer, or behaving according to some cultural and moral code of ethics employed by over 38,000 disagreeing Christian denominations. Heck if Christians can't agree on dogma what chance do they have of getting it right? The saving of the body has everything to do with the purpose for our journey in consciousness as human beings, leaving behind and evolving out of fear-based and survivalist mentalities and learning to love one another as Jesus did. Being saved is not what we think it is.

Jesus modeled a path out of fundamentalist Judaism by being hardest on the religious people, especially leaders. Jesus and John the Baptist called the religious folk *"a brood of vipers"*— terminology that is a metaphor for egocentricity or fear-based consciousness. The first appearance of this viper is of course in The Garden of Eden when the serpent spoke to Eve. Metaphorically, this is not some external enemy named Satan or Lucifer, this is our own egocentric nature speaking from within, luring us to eat the fruit of selfishness and establishing us into duality or knowing good from evil. Eating this "fruit" would begin our journey out of immortality and into time, mortality and ultimately death.

> *And the Lord God commanded the man, "You are free to eat from any tree in the garden; but you must not eat from the tree of the knowledge of good and evil, for when you eat from it you will certainly die." (Genesis 2:16-17)*

The nature of our consciousness becomes divided through egocentricity as we begin to discern and to judge between what we deem culturally as good or evil. We are beginning to understand that this journey into duality consciousness (knowing good and evil) was not a mistake but a willful decent, "falling" for a divine purpose. This fall has established mankind in time and ultimately mortality.

The day I knew that Satan was not an external foe but rather an internal function of our own egocentric consciousness changed my spiritual reality.

Now the serpent was more crafty than any of the wild animals the Lord God had made. He said to the woman, "Did God really say, 'You must not eat from any tree in the garden'?" The woman said to the serpent, "We may eat fruit from the trees in the garden, but God did say, 'You must not eat fruit from the tree that is in the middle of the garden, and you must not touch it, or you will die.'▨" "You will not certainly die," the serpent said to the woman. "For God knows that when you eat from it your eyes will be opened, and you will be like God, knowing good and evil." (Genesis 3:1-5)

The day I knew that Satan was not some external foe but rather an internal function of our own egocentric consciousness changed my spiritual reality. I had then, and still hear so much resistance to this concept because people want to blame evil on an enemy that exists *outside of themselves*.

The Old Testament chronicles the journey of our young and immature consciousness that needs rules, regulations and a God who would reflect man's own dual nature—a God we could relate to—a God that loved and hated, rewarded and punished, gave life and took life. For human consciousness to evolve, the ego needs to see an externalization of spiritual principles. This is how we learn. Therefore we have concepts of an external God, a savior, a devil, heaven and hell. But in reality, the Bible presents to us a spectacular view of our own internal landscape. Not external from us at all. The Bible presents a mystical view of our unseen human dynamics, where we were and where we are headed.

We are undergoing an incredible shift in consciousness, as the seed planted in the garden of man's consciousness through the teachings of Jesus (and other spiritual masters) is now coming into maturity. This message came to set us free from the dualist and egocentric mode of being. The New Testament represents the shift out of the law that formerly governed man's behavior in the Old Testament and into the love that is necessary if we are to progress along the path of spiritual enlightenment. Jesus said that all of the law (over six hundred requirements) now hangs on only two commandments.

Love God, Love one another as yourself. (Matthew 22:40)

These two commandments would begin to nurture this seed into germination, gently coaxing consciousness out of fear and even tyranny.

As a little girl I can clearly remember the feeling of fear that enveloped me when the preacher would give the altar call. I think I got "saved" at least three dozen times just to make sure. I would lie in bed at night thinking about the rapture and the second coming of Christ and oh how I didn't want to be left behind when it happened.

The term rapture is not found in the Bible however here is the rapture experience described in scripture:

For the Lord himself will come down from heaven, with a loud command, with the voice of the archangel and with the trumpet call of God, and the dead in Christ will rise first. After that, we who are still alive and are left will be caught up together with them in the clouds to meet the Lord in the air. And so we will be with the Lord forever. Therefore encourage one another with these words. (1 Thessalonians 14:16-18)

As we progress through the upcoming chapters we will begin to see the scriptures metaphorically. Jesus said the Kingdom (of heaven) is within you. So in the scripture above, where does the Lord come from? This scripture alludes to Divinity descending from heaven (higher consciousness) to join in union with the ascending human consciousness. These mysterious events do not occur externally. They are internal and display to us that which is unseen with the physical eye. These scriptures must be intuited and therefore we are encouraged with continual instruction from Jesus to *"lift our eyes and see."* Down throughout the ages people have waited and looked outside of themselves for these events to occur.

The theory of masses of people disappearing off of the face of the earth was popularized over a century ago and continues today. Within fundamentalism it is largely substantiated with this scripture:

> *Then there will be two men in the field; one will be taken and one will be left. Two women [will be] grinding at the mill; one will be taken and one will be left. (Matthew 24:40-41)*

I remember at gatherings we would sing a song over and over with these lyrics:

> *Two men walking up a hill one disappears and one's left standing still. I wish we'd all been ready. There's no time to change your mind, the Son has come and you've been left behind.*

We know that programming and brainwashing takes place through repetition and if I sang that song once I sang it a hundred times. We would sway and sing, and look at the friends that we brought to the meeting who were not saved and hope and pray that when the preacher gave the altar call that they would raise their hands and accept Jesus as their Lord and savior. And when they did we would weep for joy that they were safe at last. They were one of us, and speaking for myself, I felt more secure with people that believed like me. If they didn't, they became somewhat suspect and even a wee bit ostracized. Alas, I am now reaping what I have sowed. Recently I even had friends abruptly leave a social gathering when I was asked to speak of my evolving spiritual beliefs. It was a clear message to stop speaking of it or they would withhold their presence.

Let's take a look at this scripture again, this time with a metaphorical lens:

> *Then there will be two men in the field; one will be taken and one will be left. Two women [will be] grinding at the mill; one will be taken and one will be left. (Matthew 24:40-41)*

Isn't it interesting to see this scripture metaphorically—not describing an external event—this "rapture" as it has been termed, occurs internally, within our consciousness as we experience union between God the Divine, and man. Looking internally rather than externally we may see that this is describing the marriage between Divinity and the will of man. Looking deeper, the bride is the willful mind of man that is dominated by ego and the groom is Divinity or Spirit. These two are the two becoming the *One* that is *left*. The one taken is taken in marriage. The bride taken is the egocentric counterpart, the one that submits to the groom, for the union of the two becoming the *One*. The whole of Matthew 24 describes cataclysm indeed as we experience the end of duality (life as we know it) and the beginning of the *One* new creation. If we view scripture through the lens of fear and duality we will be fearful and see fearful things. I still recall vivid images of people being separated from their loved ones as they were snatched up and away from the earth because I interpreted the scriptures using fear. Through the lens of hope we see a beautiful love story where Divinity "courts" our humanity. We just need to shift out of fear.

And the two will become one flesh. 'So they are no longer two, but one. Therefore what God has joined together, let man not separate. (Mark 10:8-9)

You are not a victim; you are a participant in the greatest story ever told.

The *two becoming one* is the dualistic operating system of the human being as it yields to union or oneness. Dualism or knowing and judging between good and evil become irrelevant for those entering into the next age. Scripture alludes to this mystical marriage many times. It is the union between Divinity and man within the framework of the human being that is told within parables and stories.

Scripture, when viewed through the lens of fear will produce more schism and judgment. We are given the opportunity to *fear not* and to *lift our eyes and see.* Yes, we can see strictly historical, literal events if we want, but I was dissatisfied with what I knew and wanted to know more. This scripture foretells the end of duality, as we know it and is a harbinger for the cataclysmic changes already upon us as one age gives way to the next.

I spent the first forty-three years of my life as a fundamentalist Christian and the last twelve in search of the Divine. Come with me now to experience a great shift in consciousness, discovering that you are not a victim; you are a participant in the greatest story ever told. You, endowed with the eternal spark of Divinity, have planned a willful descent into the mortal world to ransom for yourself a helpmate. This helpmate, the human body, will support immaterial Divinity and its journey to find manifestation and expression in the physical domains of our universe and beyond. You are in the process of saving a body for your divine self.

Summary Points:

- God moves in all types of flawed systems. When miracles happen they tend to validate the flawed system.
- Divinity works even while consciousness slumbers beneath the blanket of the ego and within corrupt fear-based systems.
- Elective brainwashing is an integral part of fundamentalism.
- Redefining terminology; "Saved" does not mean that we are going to heaven when we die. To be "saved" is for the mortal to be clothed with immortality.
- The Bible generally outlines through cultural stories three levels of consciousness:

   Old Testament (old consciousness)—we see God externally and through the eyes of fear-based processes.

   The New Testament (new consciousness) represents an introduction to transitioning consciousness that is exiting the law and fear-based systems. It is here we see the manifestation of the Christ in their midst and a changing of consciousness begin.

   Book of Revelation is a detailed account of this transition culminating in the overcoming of egocentric consciousness— awakened to love and entering the *age to come*. This book travels through consciousness and vividly explains through rich metaphoric content our unfolding as participants in the perilous drama of the formation of Christ in us. Birth is not easy. The narrow way we travel in consciousness, forsaking the former egocentric mode of being is like dying; a process we are told is necessary if we are to enter into the *age to come*.

- Raising a hand and walking an aisle to accept Jesus into your heart to be "saved" is not anywhere in the Bible.
- You will pay a price debunking dogma.
- Jesus modeled a path out from religious fundamentalism.

Chapter Three

Moving From Victim to Participant— Bridging the Gap

Sometimes traumatic events propel us into unfamiliar territories in consciousness. Something happens and a veil lifts within our psyche and we are given the opportunity to see things differently. Trauma fractures the dome of our reality allowing our consciousness to seep out like a spy to see beyond the boundaries of our present perception.

I like to describe my awakening processes as happening incrementally, like the minute hand on a clock, moving around the dial. Most often I moved through perceptual changes in my spiritual walk one minute at a time; however, in 2005 I had a huge shift on my *spiritual reality clock* and in fact, I am still digesting the information that I received along with the manifestation of spiritual phenomena that is still happening as a result of this shift. The following events happened several years after my departure from church. Our whole family was catapulted into a different sphere of understanding and influence.

Christian, our middle son, was a bit of a wild child, always pushing the envelope of acceptability. He had tattoos, piercings, and blond spiked hair. I remember clearly in early 2002 when he told his father and me that he wanted to enlist in the army. 9/11 had happened just months before and Chris was adamant that this was *his destiny*. We were proud of him for knowing what he wanted to do with his life and reluctantly supported his decision.

I guess he thought he was giving me some sort of comfort when he came home from Fort Hood, Texas, prior to his deployment, sporting a new tattoo. My husband said just a few more and he could join the circus. Chris didn't think that was funny. This was back when tattoos were not so common. He took his shirt off and turned around to reveal a giant robed angel holding a sword on his back. He said, *"Don't worry Momma; while I am over there, an angel has got my back."*

He had been among the first wavers to enter the theatre of war, and was stationed in Tikrit, Iraq. At times he worked in a supply store of sorts where he was able to use instant messenger to keep in contact with us and we cherished the phone calls we would receive on occasion. He came home on leave after six months in theatre and we had a "Welcome Home, Happy Thanksgiving, Merry Christmas, Happy New Year's and Happy Birthday" party for him; all the celebrations he would miss over the next six months. By January of 2005, he finished his third year in the Army and was discharged honorably. He returned home from Iraq without a scratch. He and his girlfriend, Joanna, were engaged and life was getting back to normal. He was thinking about attending college or starting a small business in our city.

In the spring of 2005, life was extremely busy. Lyle was enrolled in the Executive MBA Program at Texas A&M University while working as the VP of Sales and Marketing for a national company. There was not a lot of free time for the two of us, but we managed to juggle life, family, work, and school. Lyle is a bit of an enigma, extremely smart and classified as gifted-genius. But emotionally he always seemed a bit behind the curve, opting for logic rather than being "touchy feely" as he puts it. He has been very good for me, providing a healthy measure of left-brained input to an acutely right-brained female.

I had been struggling, however, with bouts of what I thought was depression. For months I would at times be apprehended by a sense of dread, and I remember pleading with God, *"Please, don't let this happen."* I didn't know what *this* was, although I felt impending sorrow and despair. I think the tears that I shed during 2005 would have easily covered the bottom of a bathtub about two inches deep. When the tears came, they would not stop, sometimes for days on end. Lyle would travel some, and on those days I would turn on the tap and just let them flow, feeling that if they did not come out, I would burst.

One night in April, I woke up with a start to see Lyle sitting up abruptly in bed. Cold, clammy, and soaked with sweat, he told me of a disturbing vision: *"It wasn't a dream because it came in a flash; it was Chris in front of me, missing limbs."* He told me the vision had come the night before as well, but he did not wake me to tell me.

"What do you think it means?" he asked.

An odd question, I thought, for someone so logical to inquire about the meaning to a vision or a dream.

I replied, *"Maybe it is some kind of left-over fear from Chris being over in Iraq."*

There were always news reports on television of soldiers being hit by IED's (improvised explosive devices) and losing life or limbs, along with disturbing and horrific images. These "visions" would happen to Lyle three nights in a row, each night a flash of Christian before him sometimes missing all of his limbs, sometimes two limbs. Lyle and I were deeply disturbed by them but with Christian home safely from Iraq we didn't give them much thought. I continued to have the bouts of tears throughout the year. They had become a part of my daily routine, to let them out when it seemed I had become *too full*.

Sunday, November 13, 2005 was a beautiful, clear, fall day with lots of sunshine. My youngest son, Keith, Christian, and Lyle had planned a seventy-mile motorcycle trip to Houston, to attend a motorcycle show at Reliant Arena. I stayed behind and was having breakfast with my mom and sister when I received a phone call from Keith's phone. Odd, I thought because I knew they were riding, but when I answered, Lyle's voice was on the other end. They had been gone about an hour and a half at this point. Lyle's voice was steady as he explained to me that Chris had put his bike down, that he was okay and that he was being transported to Memorial Hermann Hospital in Houston. He said *"come"* and that Chris would need surgery and that his leg was badly broken. Lyle and Keith would continue on their motorcycles and meet me there. I told my mom and sister about the accident, and we left the restaurant right away, dropping them off and calling Joanna to retrieve her so that she could accompany me to Houston.

On the way, I told Joanna that there was only one thing in the world that Lyle would lie to me about, and it would be to understate Christian's condition. *"We need to prepare ourselves"*, I said. We were quiet on the ride there. I received a call from the surgical unit at the hospital asking for Christian's insurance information. Christian must have given them the number to my cell phone, I thought, as I knew Lyle and Keith were still en route to Houston on their motorcycles. Finding my way through the massive Houston medical center, we located Memorial Hermann Hospital and parked, and backing up into the space in the parking structure, I hit a pole. I didn't even take a look at what damage I may have caused. Walking quickly now to find the area where Christian was located, I asked the nurse at the ER admitting desk about his whereabouts. She looked discernibly pale, as she motioned for us to go toward the back so that we could see him before he went into surgery.

Approaching the opening double doors of the surgery pre-op area I heard, *"Barbara!"* It was Lyle's voice as I turned to see him and Keith approaching us. He motioned for us to step away from the surgical area and to join him at a small reception area with a kiosk. I wanted desperately to get back to see Christian, but Lyle and Keith both looked awful. We stepped to the kiosk and my eyes were glued to his face as Lyle began to speak; his knees buckled with his first words and Keith reached out to steady him.

Dread; dread is what I felt. It fell on me in a moment and coated me like thick dark paint. My throat burned with the sudden rush of adrenaline and my mouth felt like cotton.

Steadying himself as he pushed up with his arms to straighten his trembling body, Lyle breathed deep and told us, *"It's worse than I told you on the phone, Chris hit a pickup truck head on and his arm...his arm came off on impact."*

Mouth open, I froze. Joanna gasped. Then I swallowed hard and looked into his tear filled eyes, a shaky voice from somewhere within me replied,

"Lyle, your dreams..."

I was, in that moment somehow transported back several months earlier and was lying in bed next to Lyle. He was sitting up and soaked with sweat, telling me of his "visions" seeing Christian without limbs. Lyle's eyes connected with mine. The word 'connect' seems inadequate. But we remembered together the events of that night months before; it was as if we had been prepared for this. We heard our name called as they were waving us to the back to see Christian before surgery and we walked collectively, numbly in.

In the pre-op room there was blood, lots of blood, on the floor near the gurney where Christian lay. Joanna was at his right side and with his eyes closed he told her he loved her. I was standing near his feet and I felt fuzzy. Lyle motioned for me to get closer to Chris. I moved to his left side and told him I loved him and kissed his cheek, and he replied, *"I love you, Momma."* He then turned toward Joanna and pooched his lips for a kiss. Their lips touched for longer than a moment and Joanna's tears fell on Christian's face. She left them there. Attendants appeared and they wheeled him away.

The nurse told us when he arrived he was conscious and cognizant enough to give them my cell phone number. The police told Lyle and Keith that the collective speed at impact was roughly one hundred and forty miles per hour. Christian was not wearing a helmet. It was clear that he had sustained a head injury, but the nurse remarked, *"He remembered your cell phone number, that's a good sign."* She handed me a plastic drawstring bag containing his personal belongings. I opened the bag and smelled his gasoline soaked clothing and shuddered. It was Sunday in the top trauma center in Houston, and we were told to go to the ER waiting room. Families spilled out of the area into the corridor where we camped on the floor waiting for news. Lyle and Keith re-told the events of the morning:

"It was the damnedest thing", Lyle said as he blinked in disbelief through tears. *"Chris went to pass a minivan and he never came out of the oncoming lane. We clearly saw a bright red pickup truck oncoming but Chris did not, and the driver of the truck apparently did not see Chris either. I saw what was coming and I screamed when I realized that Chris was going to hit him. At the very last*

moment the truck driver yanked the wheel to his right but they impacted anyway."

The force of the impact from Christian's motorcycle tore the driver's side wheel off of the truck. Dodging the motorcycle chassis from the impact and riding through the curtain of debris, Lyle and Keith skidded to an abrupt stop. Lyle and Keith saw Christian's lifeless body lying near the side of the road and ran to him.

Lyle turned Chris over onto his back; His tongue was hanging out and to the side, and his body was...vacant. He was grayish white. There was no pulse, no blood, and no breath. His left arm was torn off, his left leg split open from hip to ankle. Lyle dropped to his knees and began to wail over Chris' body. After a few minutes, he collected himself and stood up looking around for Keith. Keith was standing nearby watching his father.

Lyle asked Keith if he was okay. He replied, *"Yes."*

However, Christian was *not there*. Lyle said that time seemed to move very slowly as he looked down at the body. Again his knees buckled and he collapsed onto Chris and this time gathered him up in his arms, wailing loudly. His sounds, he said, were "not human."

Moments passed and Lyle stood again and heard a woman's voice yelling as she ran toward him, *"I am an EMT! I am an EMT!"*

Lyle turned to her and said,

"It's too late, he is dead...We need an ambulance for his body..."

She arrived to where Christian lay and looking down at him she said,

"He is not dead."

Lyle turned abruptly to look down and saw that the color of life had returned to Christian's face and he was beginning to writhe in pain, and to bleed from his wounds. Oddly, first on the scene was this woman who happened to be an off duty EMT and her husband, an off duty fireman paramedic. Lyle and Keith turned to see her husband as he walked toward the scene having retrieved Christian's severed arm from the road. Someone had bungee cords with them and they bound up his wounds until the ambulance arrived, then a helicopter came to take him to Houston. Christian's mangled arm was packed on ice.

After Lyle and Keith filled us in on the details, we sat in silence on the floor. I eventually found words to call family members and friends to tell them. Over and hour and a half passed, then a Doctor appeared hurriedly and landed in front of me in a squat;

"Symons family?" he said.

"Yes", we replied collectively.

He said, *"Christian is in trouble up there. He has lost a lot of blood. His blood pressure is 50/20. We need to take his leg, it is badly damaged and requires a lot of surgery and Chris does not have time. He is bleeding out."*

I motioned with my arms as if to push him away and said, *"Yes. Go."* For the first time it hit us that Chris might not make it through surgery. We stared blankly at one another. Then Joanna collapsed onto my lap on the floor with a yelp.

An hour or two had passed and I paced the hallway area and waiting room wondering how would Chris be able to learn how to walk with a prosthetic leg if he did not have an arm and a hand to grip a crutch? My thoughts were jumbled and bordered on hysteria; I was projecting way out ahead. I felt nauseated. Still pacing, thoughts coming way too fast to process, and I began to feel fuzzy again. Then, I had a feeling of "lifting up."

It felt like I floated gently just a few inches above and to the right of my body and like I was standing on a pillow. The floor was not firm beneath my feet. A voice from inside of me spoke in a whisper saying, *"Barbara, remember, he chose this and so did you."*

I stood there floating and protesting silently, shaking my head, *"no."* Simultaneously, somewhere from behind, yet in me, I heard faintly, *"Yes, I remember."*

I kept blinking as if to try and process what I had just heard, although shaking my head seemed as if I gave credence to actually hearing the statement. Did I just hear a voice in my head? Did I choose this? Did he choose this? I thought, why would anyone choose something like this? Why would a mother choose this for her child? No, I shook my head from side to side but I was feeling uncertainty now. As if to try to convince myself I thought, No, he didn't choose this and neither did I. Again from within, the voice said, *"There is no human suffering in vain. All suffering produces something of great value in the Earth."*

Feeling weight on my feet again, I found myself standing in the waiting room and staring at the large salt-water aquarium in the middle of the room. The voice continued to speak to me—things of great consequence, and the information seemed to fill me like air. It said that yes we had been privy to these happenings and choices, and agreements were made. We needed to *"experience certain things that would help us in our advancing and unfolding purpose during this incarnation."* WHAT? This incarnation? I had chosen this? Made agreements? I was a rigid fundamentalist up until 1999 and was slowly coming out from the maelstrom of dogma—these thoughts were clearly *new age* and something I had not previously embraced. New age ideas were considered deception and frowned upon to read about or consider such things. But now these concepts rang true in some sense, to a part of me that was not...logically human. I did not dismiss them but let them remain within me calling upon them when I had a moment of peace outside of the anguish.

It took me months to process what was spoken to me that day. I came to understand this; as Divinity, in a place before we incarnate into physical form and are partnered with humanity, *we know things.* Before incarnation we are not within a human body, mortality or linear time and somehow our life's course is chosen; we see and get to choose our experiences, ultimately for the *collective and greater good.* Outside of time, as Divinity, we are not yet merged with the human aspect of being, we have not yet taken on human form and consciousness—especially the part of us that knows and discerns between good things and bad things or having knowledge between good and evil. After all, what logical person would choose such futile, horrific and painful things? But in and through the part of us that is eternal and Divine, all that is seen when making such choices is *purpose.* Divinity then invests itself into humanity to develop a synergistic relationship with its human counterpart while cultivating all sorts of invaluable experiences in the material world.

We are now in part, Divinity, and Divinity, knows all things. The key to accessing this information is to "still" the part of the synergy that has its basis in linear time. This part is the human mind or intellect and it needs to stop processing linear events in order to intuit things that remain unseen. This is why meditation or *being still* is finding increasing importance in our spiritual unfolding.

> *I consider that our present sufferings are not worth comparing with the glory that will be revealed in us. The creation waits in eager expectation for the Sons of God to be revealed. For the creation was subjected to futility, not by its own choice, but by the will of the one who subjected it, in hope that the creation itself will be liberated from its bondage to decay and brought into the glorious freedom of the children of God. We know that the whole creation has been groaning as in the pains of childbirth right up to the present time. Not only so, but we ourselves, who have the first fruits of the Spirit, groan inwardly as we wait eagerly for our adoption as sons, the redemption of our bodies. (Romans 8:18-23)*

The creature, the human, is subjected to these futile events not willingly, but by this eternal and Divine counterpart who makes the journey into the material world with us as us. Divinity desires to cohabit with the human soul/ego in material form and in the process of courtship, through multiple lifetimes, eventually redeems the body from its mortal state. This is a new creation that is God and man, ether and matter, and one that is fully exercised and knowledgeable in duality, the realm of good and evil. It is Divinity fully invested in mankind, wed.

I do not judge what has happened to him as evil. It just is.

As this book unfolds I hope to explain this process in more detail. This is such a BIG story and will require a great shift in how we digest information, literally or figuratively, historically or mystically, linearly or with circularity and wholeness. Once we escape the shackles of dogmatic restriction (whether you have been involved in fundamentalism or not) we are able to apprehend the mysteries that have been hidden with the parables and other mystical teaching, in plain sight.

It is necessary to understand this willful immersion of Divinity into our mortal framework. We will experience every emotion until it finds mastery and purposeful awakening. This changed my worldview dramatically. I was now seeing my son, others and myself as participants in this unfolding drama rather than as victims of circumstance. I also deeply appreciate Christian's life path and I do not judge what has happened to him as evil. It just is. Divinity longs to build its emotional escrow account immersing itself along with us through multiple lifetimes filled with the full spectrum of emotions and experiences that are absolutely necessary for our conscious evolution. Divinity within Chris has taken him on a journey of mastery. I have had brief encounters with Christian, not as my son, but seeing him as a master over his life's circumstances, gathering needed and valuable experience. I love this quote by Louisa May Alcott: *"I'm not afraid of storms, for I'm learning how to sail my ship."*

We are on a journey of mastery.

Chris is learning how to sail his "ship" and if I judge his accident as traumatic, horrible, excruciatingly painful, etc., then it will be. Judgment is creative and reinforces this present reality. We are all captains learning to sail our ships. Becoming masters over our creative potential, we must become adept at storing, focusing and releasing our emotional vibrational currency for it is the creative force that will frame and fill the age to come. We are on a journey of mastery.

Presently, we are creating and sustaining our world, albeit largely unbeknownst to us, by the unconscious focus of our thought and emotion. We are just practicing here. And thank God there is a time limit (mortality) and a purposeful "time gap" between thought, emotion and its eventual manifestation lest we really create more of a mess than we already have.

We need to get over ourselves and the circumstances we find ourselves in and recognize that we are participants, not victims.

Every emotion has an empirical value that moves the quantum world of matter quite effectively. From the movement of butterfly wings, to the movement of tectonic plates, every emotion we employ has value and moves something—yes the Earth moves because of us. There is a glorious future ahead for the awakened human being, aware that it is endowed with Divinity; such are called the Sons of God. The power and means to create worlds consciously, effectively, efficiently and *without end* is within them. We need to get over ourselves and the circumstances we find ourselves in and recognize that we are participants, not victims.

I regularly walk Harry, our Great Dane, at a local park. One day on our way into the park we came across a rather large turtle, about the size of a cantaloupe that was stuck between the street and the curb. It had been trying to climb when its shell became lodged vertically on the concrete curb. Stuck between places its little feet were dog paddling in the air but unable to reach any surface at all. There it was, almost vertical to the curb with the hind part of its shell resting on the concrete street. When we approached, the turtle instinctively withdrew into its shell. Harry sniffed at it curiously as I thought long and hard about moving the little guy and finally reached down and with careful attention positioned my fingers around the shell and away from its mouth. I lifted it upward and heard a threatening growl-type noise from within the shell and I laughed and said, *"Oh shut up. I am just trying to help you."*

I set the turtle down in the grass beyond the curb, smiled to myself and thought; *sometimes we just need help getting over ourselves*. Immediately I had this sense of wonder knowing that I had just experienced another life lesson.

When I teach these concepts at conferences I encounter people all over the country processing the words, *"You are not a victim; you are a participant."* For some, the light comes on and they weep with joy. Others remain in their salty wash of tears and helpless victimhood. It is vital that we understand the necessity for us to become well acquainted with the full spectrum of emotions from despair to joy, each one adding to the priceless value of our vibrational escrow account. The Apostle Paul said that his body was lacking in the afflictions of Christ and so he rejoiced in his sufferings.

> *Now I rejoice in my sufferings for your sake, and fill up on my part that which is lacking of the afflictions of Christ in my flesh. (Colossians 1:24)*

Wow. Paul understood the purpose in suffering and recognized that the corporeal body must "fill up" where the valuable experience of affliction is lacking. The afflictions of "Christ" are the experiences that the Divine experiences along with its human counterpart that are necessary to become adept at the movement and distribution of our emotional currency. The body of Christ (collective humanity) must experience all things good and evil. After all, we can't create a beautiful tapestry with just one color of thread, can we?

The term "victim" offers restriction while the word "participant" offers liberty. Victim has helpless energy attached to it while participant implies empowerment, a knowing of, and agreement to, circumstances even though most people may perceive them as negative. Even for those who have experienced rape, terror and other horrific experiences, I have seen them re-frame traumatic events and transition from a place of despair and into hope. I have watched them migrate out from seeing and perceiving as a mere human, to understanding *as Divinity*. If they can see past their individual circumstances and understand that there is a purpose for such darkness, then those same will truly know what it means to forgive. For theirs is a holistic view and they are forgiving their human-hood immersed in and subjected to futility and understanding purpose in ALL things both light and dark.

It is necessary to forgive—not just individual circumstances but the totality of our human-hood. Those that do are awakening Divinity within the housing of the human. They choose to see with the single eye that manifests a holistic view when in union with the Divine rather than the fractured view that comes from duality and helplessness.

> *The light of the body is the eye: if therefore thine eye be single, thy whole body shall be full of light. (Matthew 6:22)*

We must transition into unity for unity offers light, not the darkness of duality. Humanity alternates between broad sweeping stages of light and darkness, day and night. The daytime (light) is when we are given information and the nighttime (darkness) is when this information is applied and valuable experiences are learned. We have been in an egocentric/ego-dominant night. It is time to do a morning stretch and enter into the dawn of a new era where everything is perceived differently when there is LIGHT.

> *Though he were a Son, yet learned he obedience by the things which he suffered; And being made perfect, he became the author of eternal salvation unto all them that obey him; Called of God a high priest after the order of Melchizedek, of whom we have many things to say, and hard to be uttered, seeing ye are dull of hearing. For when for the time ye ought to be teachers, ye have need that one teach you again which be the first principles of the oracles of God; and are become such as have need of milk, and not of strong meat. For every one that uses milk is unskillful in the word of righteousness: for he is a babe. **But strong meat belongs to them that are of full age, even those who by reason of use have their senses exercised to discern both good and evil.** (Hebrews 5:8-14)*

> *Therefore leaving the principles of the doctrine of Christ, let us go on unto perfection. (Hebrews 6:1)*

There is so much that can be seen in this scriptural example. Let's focus on the part that references consuming *strong meat*. Strong meat is a metaphor for, and is synonymous with, learning about the *Melchizedek order of immortal beings*. Our senses must be

41

exercised or proficient in the knowledge of good and evil, or duality consciousness, if we are to understand and transition into the mechanics that drive the realm of immortality. It is in fact a *prerequisite for perfection* or ascension. We must become well acquainted in the age where duality thrives before we are able to transcend the age and digest the meat or information regarding the Melchizedek order. It is this age where Divinity has chosen to receive its education in the material world from within the mortal framework, the human being. It is also in this age where human emotions are cultivated and projected albeit presently unconscious, to sustain reality. To some degree there has been a grand manipulation of mass consciousness by keeping the human projecting negatively. Negativity maintains duality, that is, the realm of good and evil, reality, as we know it. But, our suffering is not in vain. It is highly productive until the time of awakening and enlightenment. This realm is our school.

The Buddha says, *"Enlightenment is the end of suffering."* We suffer only when we desire something other than what we have. And we have desire because we judge and discern between good and evil. It is through our judgment between good and evil then, that reality, as we know it is sustained. Therefore, to transition the age, judgment must cease.

Bridging the Gap

Twenty-eight units of blood and eight units of plasma later, Chris made it through surgery and we could only wait for him to wake up. It would be four long days before he regained consciousness. During those four days, I heard that internal voice again, this time saying, *"Bridge the gap!"*

What? What does that mean? What gap? I was not sure what this meant, what this task required, but the voice had my undivided attention. I was sure it had something to do with Christian, and why he had ultimately *chosen* this experience. Pacing around his bed in the STICU (shock-trauma-intensive-care-unit) I prayed, cried, and wrung my hands in quiet desperation.

"Wake up, Christian! Wake up!" I cried, repeatedly.

"Bridge the Gap!" I heard again

"But I don't know what that means! Help me!" I pleaded.

Looking back I am not sure about my state of mind—I was, it seemed, in a heightened emotional state of hysteria for days on end. I shook continually, was sleep deprived and was hearing this voice in my head, telling me things that I did not fully understand.

The following morning I was walking the corridor between campuses at Memorial Hermann Hospital. It was during shift change and I was walking amidst a sea of scrubs. I kept my head down, my eyes horribly swollen from crying. Once, looking up, I saw a man walking toward me, way down the corridor, who had to be well over six and a half feet tall because he was at least a head taller than most. He had an unusual cadence about his walk, a mop for a head of hair flopping from side to side as he swaggered closer. As the sea of people intermittently parted, I saw glimpses of his long lanky body, and became aware that he was wearing a shirt that had the familiar word "GAP" printed on it. *"Bridge the Gap!"* I remembered. I grinned and thought, okay, nice synchronicity, but there must be thousands of those shirts in Houston. My smile faded and I continued on my way, keeping an occasional eye on this unusual guy. As he got closer I glanced up and noticed that he was looking directly at me. I looked down abruptly a little embarrassed that he had seen me looking at him. Now with my head up again, he was closer still, and I saw that there were two more words on his shirt, much smaller and above the word "gap." He was walking in front of and then beside me, still looking directly into my eyes. I lowered my eyes to read his shirt and it said, "Bridge the GAP." My mouth dropped open. He smiled, still looking at me as he passed by, and tears, once again, started falling down my cheeks. I have come to understand that messengers and signs are everywhere speaking to us. It is synchronicity at its best.

So what is this mysterious GAP? Over the next several months, I came to understand many things about the gap. Among other things, the gap is a purposeful "dead zone" in consciousness that lies between dimensions. It is like the buffer zone between heaven and earth, much like the Earth's atmosphere (troposphere, stratosphere and mesosphere) separates the earth from outer space; earth representing our logic-based intellect and heaven representing our intuitive faculties. This microcosmic gap in consciousness between our intellect and intuition is reflected in the macrocosmic gap, the dead-zone between earth and outer space and also in the expanse between dimensions. It is the gap that stands between human logic and Divine intuition. It is also the gap that stands between time and no time, mortality and immortality. It is the gap that stands between the natural and the supernatural, between the mundane and the miraculous. I see the gap in many places within our human perception. These gaps need a bridge for human consciousness to migrate over, out from fear, duality and limitation and into unity.

In the human brain between the hemispheres there is a gap, a flat layer of tissue made up of neural fibers called the corpus callosum. It connects the left and right cerebral hemispheres and is believed to facilitate inter-hemispheric communication. Mystically, it is what holds duality in place, separating the two halves of the brain like "No Man's Land." During wartime, No Man's Land is a narrow expanse of land between and separating front line trenches that is unoccupied. It stands between two conflicting viewpoints, value systems or opinions.

This gap in consciousness has helped form human perception into the sensory world of dualism. In the proverbial Garden of Eden, mankind "ate" from the Tree of the Knowledge of Good and Evil or duality consciousness, and saw one another as unclothed or separate from the Divine. Having been introduced to fear, self-focus and uncertainty by the serpent (our egocentric nature) we now function largely out of the logical part of the brain—the left or western hemisphere that has been separated from the right or eastern intuitive hemisphere of the brain by the corpus callosum. This perspective in dualism is created by the five physical senses as the human being continually judges between what it perceives by them.

There is a phrase from Hermetic philosophy that says, *"As below so above, as above so below"* that is often quoted to relay the understanding that the macrocosm often reflects the microcosm and vice versa.

The left or "western" hemisphere of the brain reflects logic and intellect. Interestingly, the Earth's western hemisphere is generally based in logic and linear intelligence or intellect.

The right or "eastern" hemisphere of the brain reflects imagination and intuition—the Earth's eastern hemisphere is generally more mystical and intuitive.

We see patterns emerge in our physical Earth that generally reflect the inner workings of consciousness. The coming evolutionary leap will be a bridge built between the two halves of the brain that will yield a greater synergy than what we presently have. This bridge will herald the ability to shift out from duality consciousness and into union. I find it interesting that at one time all of the landmasses of our earth were connected but through time have separated sometimes leaving a vague land bridge below the surface of the waters. It is the same thing in consciousness. Although we separate from one another via various cultures, idealism, politics and religion, we are still ONE human race.

Presently we function primarily from the intellect or left brain but soon we will become more and more able to employ our right hemisphere or intuitive brain. This shift is out from the intellect and egocentric dominated ways of thinking and processing information and into the intuitive center of our consciousness. I might even say it is moving from literalism to mysticism. Presently the vast majority of humanity is stuck in fear-based systems. We are made to focus on right and wrong; reward and punishment; love and hate; good and evil. This grounds us in the intellect.

We are about to shift beyond this scratch in the record so to speak, and will move into a completely different dispensation of awareness. This movement of consciousness will give us access beyond our five senses into the intuited realms of the unseen.

At some point during our evolutionary journey, this gap was purposely forged within human consciousness, not unlike the metaphorical parting of the Red Sea. Water is representative of human consciousness. Moses (who is a metaphor for corporeal human consciousness under the control of the ego) journeys through the divided sea (metaphorically forming the gap of dualism between logic and intuition) and into the wilderness wanderings of limited human intellect. He leads and provides the law for the egocentric human as it navigates duality unconscious and unaware that it is imbued with the Spark of the Divine. This sojourning into dualism was necessary so that the human and Divinity would be well invested into the processes of creating through dualism, utilizing thought propelled by emotion, the two components essential for creating reality.

The task to *bridge the gap* is to provide an enhanced pathway of understanding that allows for the navigation across the logic-based part of the brain, through the corpus callosum, that is, what is commonly referred to as the "veil" and into the intuitive, mystical area of consciousness. It is from this position that the Spirit leads us rather than being tossed about by limited human reasoning. In cultural symbolism the bride's veil is lifted in marriage (union). This area of our consciousness is not couched in linear time and is what Eckhart Tolle so effectively teaches us to touch through stillness in his book, *The Power of Now*. The egocentric led mind must keep still if it is to hear the gentle voice of the Divine within. It is the bride yielding to the groom.

This whole process is metaphorically *coming out from wandering in the wilderness,* from desert into the Promised Land of immortality that flows with milk and honey. It must be noted that milk is the food of babes or our limited, logic based mind; and honey is a food that never perishes, a metaphor for Divinity. The pineal gland (intuitive sight), when functioning optimally, secretes a milky white fluid along with a gold colored substance. This "land" or optimal state of being provides milk and honey—sustenance for both aspects, human and Divine now functioning in tandem and balance. We are migrating out from left brained intellect/logic/egocentric/duality consciousness and into right-brained intuition where the Spirit within guides and directs rather than the self-focused ego. It is the left-brain that largely judges between good and evil, right and wrong. We have for too long been dominated by logic and as such, we have been wandering in a type of conscious wilderness. A leap through this wilderness is taking place, as a pathway is being created, so that human thought may originate from our intuitive mind and then enlists logic to see any creative process through to fruition. It is movement from right to left or from east to west. Isn't it interesting that Hebrew script is written and read from right to left?

In studies when the brain is wired with electronic devices to detect activity, the individual hemispheres of the brain flash like a lightning storm depending on what kind of stimuli is offered. Intuitive stimuli cause right (eastern) hemisphere illumination. Logical stimuli cause left (western) hemisphere illumination.

In Matthew 24, Jesus warned that there would be those who would say the Christ was appearing in a field or in a building (externally or man-made structures) and he said this: *"Do not believe them."* I think that is because the Christ is being formed within us and is an amalgamation of the Divine and man. The Christ's appearing will be within man. The Christ will not be found in the form of one man but will be a corporeal man. He also said this about the coming or the culmination of the human into god-hood:

> *For false Christs and false prophets will appear and perform great signs and miracles to deceive even the elect—if that were possible. See, I have told you ahead of time. So if anyone tells you, "There he is, out in the desert," do not go out; or, "Here he is, in the inner rooms," do not believe it. For as lightning that comes from the east is visible even in the west, so will be the coming of the Son of Man. (Matthew 24:24-27)*

Metaphorically I see this as when thought originates in the east (intuition, inspiration) and is visible in the west (logic) then we will see a dramatic change in human consciousness and indeed the "coming" of the Son of Man, the prodigal returning to his Father's *home*. No longer driven by human and dualistic logic and intellect, the Divine within will inspire our every move. We will see the manifestation of the transitioning Son of Man to the Christ in our midst, within the *"clouds"* of human consciousness. This is the metaphorical *"pearl of great price"* and the *"treasure in earthen vessels" (Matthew 13:46, 2 Corinthians 4:7)* that Jesus referred to. This pearl is Christ consciousness that has been forming within the human for ages. This pearl will enable humanity to rise above all limitation imposed through duality so that the mundane world of mortality ascends to the miraculous domain of the immortal. Mortality offers us dis-ease, distortion, sickness, limitation and death. Our pattern set through Jesus shows us that nothing, no-thing is impossible. Blind eyes opened, withered limbs grew and the dead were raised to life. *"Oh you of little faith!"* he said. We must believe in who and what we are and this bridge will be built.

Things do not happen to you; they happen for you.

It is this "gap" between logic and intuition that I am called to bridge. I feel this also means to bring the metaphorical (intuitive understanding) of the mystical script found within parables and other texts, to light. If we interpret literally, we miss the mystery of the "coming" of Christ. This has been the main impetus in my journey coming out of fundamentalism. Literalism has left the building. It has become difficult not to see the symbolism that surrounds us. We must begin the journey out of history and enter into mystery. Throughout this material I will bring metaphoric interpretation into focus to help bridge the gap between logic and our intuitive mind using language and imagery.

It is vital to understand that as participants in this unfolding drama we have an elevated view to grasp the purpose for experiencing good and evil. Victimhood plants you squarely into duality whereas being a participant catapults you into understanding the creative processes of the age to come. No matter what has happened in your life you must remember this—*these things do not happen to you; they happen for you.* We are transitioning in consciousness out of this passing age and into the next. Come with me, over the expanse of the gap and help me build the bridge into the age to come!

Years after his accident, Chris came over rather ecstatic one day, pulled off his shirt and told me to *"really look"* at his angel tattoo.

I shrugged my shoulders and said,

"It looks like your angel tattoo."

He said emphatically, *"No, mom, really LOOK at it, what do you see, or better yet, what do you NOT see?"*

I was amazed when he pointed out to me that the angel tattoo was actually missing a hand and a foot just as he is now. It had never been tattooed in place.

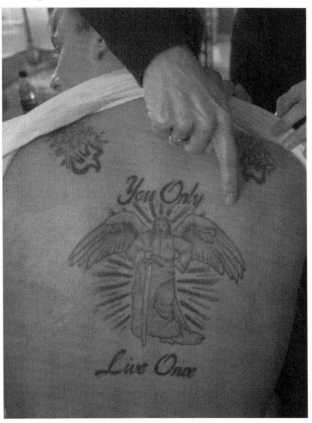

Christian is a warrior of sorts. An angel called to manifest in his flesh the power of the age to come. Ironically, named Christian, I see him an archetype for Christianity to rise above the mundane and to enter into the miraculous. He is not a victim of circumstance—he is a Divine participant in this human drama helping humanity cross over into the age to come.

Wake up Christian!

Summary Points:

- Trauma is the harbinger of change.

- We choose the path that will cause us to awaken and sometimes that path includes trauma.

- When we choose our life experiences we are not yet human and therefore do not judge future experiences to be good or evil—all we see is purpose and what our life's circumstances will produce in us.

- All suffering produces something of great value.

- We chose our unique path and every experience matters and adds to our emotional and vibrational escrow.

- Emotions are a type of currency.

- Divinity has willfully invested itself into our mortal framework.

- We are participants not victims.

- We create and sustain our world by focusing thought and emotion and presently we do it unconsciously.

- Time serves as a buffer between thought, emotion and its ultimate manifestation.

- The body of Christ (collective humanity) must experience all things good and evil. We can't create a beautiful tapestry with just one color of thread.

- It is necessary to forgive—not just individual circumstances but the totality of your human-hood.

- In order for the mortal to transition into immortality the same must be fully exercised to discern good and evil—it is in fact a prerequisite.

- Leaving human understanding we must bridge the gap, the expanse that stands between human logic and Divine intuition.

- The [second] coming of Christ will not be outside of you. Its appearing is within the human being.

- Things do not happen to you; they happen for you.

Phase Two

Shifting Consciousness

Chapter Four

The New Wineskin and Un-shrunk Cloth. Exchanging Old Consciousness for New

Countless books were written about the anticipated cataclysm slated to occur on or before December 21st, 2012. This was the end of the Mayan Calendar and many prophecies from various cultures foretold of a world event happening on this date. I, along with many others, saw this event as heralding a great shift in consciousness that would provide the springboard for major changes in our world. Now that we have successfully navigated past 2012 it is important to note a change in our world's consciousness. I believe wholeheartedly that we experienced a profoundly smooth shift. It could have been worse. Just as when shifting gears in an automobile, an inexperienced driver can make the process a bit jerky. We have moved through this change with little fanfare as more and more people are finding the "center" in consciousness, refusing to be polarized by cultural ideology, religion and politics. More and more are bridge builders choosing love, tolerance and acceptance over judgment; all are appropriate states of consciousness that are required if we are to transition into the advancing age. As a part of a book proposal endorsement my editors said the following about my material:

> *"These messages are not only timely at this stage of human evolution, but also necessary to help the millions out there who struggle to incorporate outdated and ineffective interpretations of religion in a society that no longer wishes to support fear and judgment within their spiritual practices."*

Fear and judgment have been the primary and motivating drivers of this passing age and humanity has been held captive by/and addicted to it. But fear will not support the expansive consciousness now emerging upon the planet. The restrictive nature of fear is giving way to expanding love. In the scripture below Jesus spoke of the coming of *"the kingdom"* to Earth (which translates as the merging of the next dimensional level with our present level) and gave us instruction on how to deal with the ramifications of such a coming:

> *No one sews a patch of un-shrunk cloth on an old garment, for the patch will pull away from the garment, making the tear worse. Neither do men pour new wine into old wineskins. If they do, the skins will burst, the wine will run out and the wineskins will be ruined. No, they pour new wine into new wineskins, and both are preserved. (Matthew 9:16-17)*

It is interesting that Jesus used these two contradicting metaphors, *un-shrunk cloth* and the *new wine* and *wineskin* for his teaching. New wine expands but un-shrunk cloth has the opposite quality—it contracts.

Present day harbingers of change will be resisted by the religious order of the day.

Jesus spoke mainly to those that wanted to learn but at the same time there were those that resisted him and his teaching in the crowds, those who were a part of the religious order of the day and even accused him of blasphemy. Jesus came as a revolutionary, bucking the system of the law, breaking the rules of long held traditions within the belief structure of Judaism. In the same way, modern harbingers of change will be resisted by religious adherents of the present day.

Referring to himself, or at the very least to his teaching, Jesus said that *you cannot sew a new piece of un-shrunk cloth on an old garment* and *you cannot put new wine into an old wineskin.* An old wineskin has already been filled with wine and has gone through the fermentation process and has stretched and expanded as far as it can. Pouring new, volatile and still fermenting wine into it will compromise the skin and cause it to rupture as it expands with the fermenting wine. The new wineskin (let's make the comparison to consciousness that has shifted out of fear) will have the ability to move with the ever expanding multi-dimensional and intuitively discerned world that Jesus spoke of (new wine). By speaking in parables Jesus was trying to shift the way that they thought. He was speaking to their intuitive mind. Literalism would no longer serve their developing consciousness, as it is one dimensional and restrictive. Jesus, through his teaching, brought them multidimensional information necessary for them to evolve spiritually as they began their migration out from limitation and into expansion, out from mortality and into the possibilities of an endless life. Paul said this:

> *He has made us competent as ministers of a new covenant—not of the letter but of the Spirit; for the letter kills, but the Spirit gives life. (2 Corinthians 3:6)*

I am comparing the letter and the Spirit to literalism and mysticism. If we interpret the scriptures literally or by the letter, we are told that it brings *death (and are we mortal?)*. If we interpret scriptures mystically or metaphorically we will find the secrets of immortal life hidden within the text. However, the early church slid into misconduct and control through fear and intimidation and looked little like the New Testament Church. The Dark Ages emerged and the message of Jesus eventually became tainted with the blood of the Crusades. But just as a dormant seed springs to life with rain, the seed that has been planted in consciousness is springing to life today.

There seems to be so much fear of letting go of literalism in large part because it shakes the whole egocentric religious system. Heaven, hell and the devil once seen as external can now be seen mystically and archetypically by those with a *"new wineskin"* that is, the ability and desire to hear an expanded understanding of scripture. One might even say we are transitioning out of *hell* because we are no longer seeing ourselves as separate from the Divine but that indeed the Divine dwells within.

So many people in fundamentalism rigidly adhere to literal interpretation and as such end up withholding the life sustaining breath of Spirit through metaphor from their lungs. As we ready ourselves for the next leap on our spiritual, evolutionary ladder we will need flexibility. To acquire the new wineskin means letting go of all rigid and fear-based beliefs defined by various religions through literalism. For those never within fundamentalism it may be time to look at these mysterious teachings of Jesus with new eyes, scriptures not tarnished from the *continuing crusades* to convert the masses to an irrelevant system. Jesus would not do such things. His teachings were non-discriminate and inclusionary. Jesus was not trying to start a religion—He was trying to help us escape from them.

As stated previously, new wine expands but un-shrunk cloth has the opposite quality—it contracts. If one sews a new piece of cloth (that has not been pre-shrunk) onto an old garment that has been washed many times, once washed again, the old fabric will tear as the new cloth shrinks and settles into place. I had to ask myself why would Jesus use two contradicting metaphors to describe the same qualities of a new consciousness?

When I posed this question to my husband he asked me, *"Well, what expands and contracts?"*

Immediately I saw lungs, taking in precious air to sustain the body and exhaling carbon dioxide to cleanse the body. There must be an exchange—in with the new consciousness and out with the old consciousness. The old had its purpose to sustain the body but when it is time to expel the old, we must, in order to draw in the new. In understanding these two examples, the old wineskin and the old fabric cannot sustain *movement*. The teaching that Jesus brought to us is volatile and will challenge old and outdated fear-based consciousness. Fear equals limitation and restriction and there comes a time when expanding consciousness will no longer subject itself to fear. I saw that within the religious system, like a child with a bully, someday you risk being bloodied for your freedom. I have repeatedly seen first-hand how old friends, still within fundamentalism, recoil from, strike, ridicule and accuse those transitioning out of the system of everything evil. They simply cannot contain the new consciousness with an old consciousness, new wine with an old skin.

I love the picture that the oxbow lake provides. An oxbow lake forms when a river overflows its banks. When the river recedes, the oxbow lake remains but is cut off from the continual flow of the source and as such its waters turn putrid. Most religions are metaphorical oxbow lakes. It is akin to the limited intellectual mind and its attempt to know via their ego, that which is unknowable to it. Only when the ego makes the conscious decision to yield to the mind's ability to intuit truth, can it know the Divine and more importantly, the Divine within. This is reconnecting with the source of all.

One of the most painful things I experienced as I transitioned out of my fundamentalist church structure was the loss of friends and colleagues I had formed close ties with. As I began to embrace the metaphysical and metaphorical aspect of my spirituality, a lot of my friends turned chilly towards me and some went so far as to even avoid eye contact when they saw me in public. It was the damnedest thing. I have to say I was deeply disillusioned and disappointed in church and church people.

I had just a few friends that remained and I felt the need to cultivate and nurture those that stuck by me; Molly being one of them. We were not close as friends can be but we connected on a spiritual level. I told Lyle that I longed for a deeper connection with her and so I decided to invite her over for a visit. Ironically, Molly called that same day and asked to stop by. We exchanged polite talk and I invited her into the family room. She sat on the edge of the overstuffed leather couch, hands folded in her lap as I began to talk to her about a book that we both had been reading. Suddenly she held her hand up as if to stop me from speaking. I obliged with silence looking at her intently wondering what was wrong. Molly began to tell me that she could no longer associate with me, that I had stepped too far outside the Christian "box." I was shocked because up until that point, she'd been transitioning out of the church system as well. A few weeks later in an email exchange I asked her why she had come to that decision and she replied by quoting scripture about only knowing Christ and him crucified *(1 Corinthians 2:2)*. According to Molly I was not giving Jesus the proper place as my Lord and Savior by questioning the *Christian idea of him*. Her answers were, it seemed, rehearsed. Many Christians will quote that scripture when doctrinally challenged.

Being ostracized and the subsequent loss of friends and even family is a frequent occurrence for those leaving fundamentalism. In fact this can occur anytime someone experiences a leap of consciousness, moving from one set of beliefs to a more expansive view. I see and hear about this all the time. For some reason, Christians separate from one another when their beliefs do not coincide with each other.

With humor, Atlanta Pastor D.E. Paulk recalls the events that split his Uncle's church in the Atlanta area decades ago:

> *"When the civil rights movement hit, the African Americans were allowed in to fellowship but half the white people left. Then when gay people were allowed in half the African Americans left. And when people of other religious persuasions were allowed in half the gay people left."*

Thankfully, human consciousness is breaking free from these biased, intolerant and limited mindsets. One cannot call himself or herself a follower of Jesus Christ and continually speak of union and oneness while manifesting division. It is written that Jesus came to bring division *(Matthew 10:34)* and so Christianity feels that it is necessary to separate from others that they deem different—too different from them. However, I think the scripture points to exactly what I said is happening—when Christ begins to manifest in our midst, the ego is very threatened and retreats, accuses and separates *itself*. However, the message of Christ is *union*. My experience is not unlike many who have found themselves disenfranchised from the church. I left emotionally battered and bruised and with my standing within the Christian community in shambles. For years I was like the man who tried to re-gather the windblown feathers of a tattered reputation. Tattered is probably an understatement. I was ruined by rumor, innuendo, half-truths and untruths. At the end of the day however, people believe what they want to believe and the loss of such friends were not really friends at all; in retrospect they were, in fact, my greatest teachers.

The New Wineskin and Un-shrunk Cloth
Exchanging Old Consciousness for New

I believe that if there was no restrictive structure like the environment of a womb, the baby would not be birthed, so who can despise the structural limitation that gave them life? Within the womb is great restriction. There comes a time when the baby can no longer "fit" inside and begins to push its way out along with the forceful contractions of the mother's uterus. When the baby enters into the birth canal, it is a time of great trauma, but even the trauma serves a purpose. Entering this compression chamber or the *"narrow way"* is when the water (metaphorically representing human consciousness) is squeezed out or expelled from the baby's lungs and it begins to breathe differently. What beautiful symbolism! This same form of church system rejected Christ too and expelled him from their midst. So threatening was his message to the status quo that they sought to kill him. If you view his life mystically rather than historically you will see a pattern emerge of our own path as we shed this passing age of law and enter into the press or narrow way of new beginnings. Religious systems will be threatened and you will be rejected.

At times in our lives we serve as the role of the womb within the mother; other times we are the one that is being born. It depends on what we have *signed up for* within that particular time of our life. Sometimes we are the student and other times we are the teacher. Having this understanding paves the way for true forgiveness. We are all just trying to walk one another home on this path we call life.

With rejection and dissolving friendships I can choose to remain in the pain of it all, re-hashing the injustices that seem to grow with each passing day; or I can see myself as a participant, not a victim, with the understanding that I am here to learn and I am in need of good teachers. It is forgiveness to bless those that have served as my teachers—lord knows at times I have not been a good student.

Those still within structured religion are divinely positioned and fulfill their present role. Mankind is endowed with the Spark of the Divine and we grow according to individually chosen timelines as well as having different perspectives that lead to conclusions about reality. I am writing about these things in hopes of expanding your thinking beyond present boundaries. There are those people that have ears to hear, and those that will not or cannot hear...yet.

The new patch and new wineskin are great metaphors for the movement that comes from awakening human consciousness. With my friend, Molly, I had tried to pour expanded spiritual concepts into an old wineskin or mindset. It doesn't work, and as a matter of fact, it caused schism. It was wrong for me to try and gain consensus in my awakening process and was no better than proselytizing within Christianity. It is good to trust the process of Divinity working within all people. With our hands we cannot form the pearl within the oyster—it happens organically. All of humanity will awaken when we have had enough sleep. Now, when the scripture exhorts us to go preach the Good News, we would be wise to follow Saint Francis of Assisi, who said,

"Preach the Gospel, if necessary, use words."

After all, the good news of the gospel message is that consciousness is liberating itself from fear and is manifesting Christ. Wise and persuasive words are for the ego and in this next growth phase in consciousness, words won't get us all the way there. This is not an intellectual process.

My message and my preaching were not with wise and persuasive words, but with a demonstration of the Spirit's power. (1 Corinthians 2:4)

In his video, *The Mayan Calendar Comes North*, Ian Xel Lungold tells us that the (intellectual/egocentric) mind is limited and in the days to come if we do not develop our intuition it will be like taking a donkey (the ego driven intellect) for a Sunday drive hitched to the back of the family station wagon traveling seventy miles per hour. The new wineskin is a parallel to our intuitive mind. The symbol of the donkey (the old wineskin) tells us that the intellectual, ego-driven mind has a speed limit. Eventually and willingly the finite mind must submit to its infinite counterpart, the intuitive or to the environment of Divinity.

Ironically, Jesus rode this beast of burden, a donkey, into Jerusalem where he was crucified. It is written that the donkey had never been ridden before—a parallel for the concept of "virgin" (covered in more detail later). But in the book of Revelation, we see that the Christ triumphantly returns on a white horse, the ego, as it has been reborn as servant to the greatest of all, and in union with the Divine within. The ego navigates through this life of futility and eventually and willingly submits to crucifixion. Then it goes into the ground for burial once and for all as master of the body and then resurrects to have its "born again" experience as servant to the Divine. This symbol of crucifixion is our journey into the material world of the earth as egocentric beings, our life and subsequent submission to the greater aspect of the Spirit, the intuitive, the Divine within.

The ego navigates through this life of futility, eventually and willingly submits to crucifixion.

The parabolic teaching of the new wineskin is an interesting take of what happens when presenting the finite mind with infinite ideas. The intellectual, ego-driven mind cannot possibly contain the wealth of knowledge and understanding that comes from intuition or Spirit. It was necessary for Jesus to speak in mysterious parables because the consciousness of that time period could not contain the truth in plain language. He recognized that it might cause a tear in the fabric of our fragile, immature, and collective consciousness. The world was not mature enough for such truth and also had yet to take the necessary plunge (baptism) into the dark ages. Jesus was clearly a being from another order that carried a frequency about him that enabled him to rise above our physical laws. Jesus was not bound by our reality and frequently moved in what we call the miraculous. He is our pattern, our way-maker that visited us when we needed him most. He knew the path we were about to embark upon and he knew that we were going to need a pattern for ascension and resurrection—just like he needed when he attended the school of Earth. He came now as an *archetypical* messiah to seed the Earth with new consciousness, demonstrating to us our own future.

Jesus embodied the new wineskin. The energy field within and around his being was superior to what was found in the typical human. Jesus was from the immortal order of Melchizedek Priests *(Hebrews 5, 6 & 7)*. Melchizedek Priests are given the charge to be an intermediary, that is, to have the ability to bridge the gap (dead zone) between the Divine and man, and as such, move inter-dimensionally. Melchizedek is an inter-dimensional being. Jesus was both Divinity and man and modeled for us our future form both physically and spiritually. He came to set the pattern of the enlightened human being that is seeded with Christ consciousness. Many parables and teachings of Jesus allude to this mysterious planting such as:

The Mustard Seed - Mark 4:31, Matthew 13:31, Luke 13:19

The Treasure Hidden in a Field - Matthew 13:44

The Pearl of Great Price - Matthew 13:46

The Leaven in the Dough - Matthew 13:33

The Growing Seed - Mark 4:26

The Sower - Mark 4:8, Luke 8:5

Jesus came and demonstrated another dimension or age out of time itself, the new creation that man would eventually become. He is a pattern for us to follow. It is said of Jesus that he is *"the firstborn of many brothers."*

For those God foreknew he also predestined to be conformed to the image of his Son, that he might be the firstborn among many brothers. (Romans 8:29)

The teachings of Jesus were like new wine in an old skin; His level of consciousness could not be understood or contained by the collective level of consciousness present on the earth during that time period. The religious status quo was very threatened and opted to try and subdue the messenger. Little did they know that their plot to kill the Christ was part of a larger pattern that if viewed holistically and metaphorically, models our own journey to the cross as the ego willingly surrenders its life of self to death and then resurrects to become a servant to the Divine within.

To see the pattern in the life of Jesus will help us see the two distinct ages present in the New Testament, both ages with completely different modes of being. One is the consciousness of the transitioning human out from the Law and the other Jesus manifested the kingdom dimension as a completed human, a new creation that was both Divinity and man residing and functioning in tandem, union, synergistically within his body.

He said in *John 14:7 "If you have seen me you have seen the father."*

Jesus had no trouble seeing his equality with the Divine.

Let this mind be in you, which was also in Christ Jesus: Who, being in the form of God, thought it not robbery to be equal with God: But made himself of no reputation, and took upon him the form of a servant, and was made in the likeness of men: And being found in fashion as a man, he humbled himself, and became obedient unto death, even the death of the cross. (Philippians 2:5-8)

As a functioning god-man, Jesus was not limited to the physical laws that this present dimension demands. We see him doing all sorts of supernatural acts and if viewed holistically, even these physical acts can be seen metaphorically. Jesus walking on water can be seen as Jesus walking above human reason as water metaphorically represents human consciousness. And better than that, he bids us to come join Him.

History? Yes! Mystery? Absolutely! The Bible even refers to Old Testament events as this:

These things happened to them as examples for you upon whom the end of the age has come. (1 Corinthians 10:11)

And the scripture compares itself to "allegory" at least five times. (Ezekiel 17:2, Galatians 4:24, Proverbs 1:6, John 10:6 and John 16:29). So we must view some, if not all of scripture as having metaphorical or allegorical value.

Within the lifetime of Jesus we see a pattern emerge of our unfolding journey in consciousness. He was a boy who became a man—we are spiritually immature babes who become mature beings. He was a man who was tempted in every way, yet overcame the realm of the egocentric self. We are likewise tempted and are in the process of awakening to overcome our egocentric self. He died to his will, *"Nevertheless not my will but thy will be done" (Luke 22:42)* and went to the cross willingly where his humanity intersected his Divinity and ultimately demonstrated through resurrection as an immortal god-man. Today, humanity is at such a crossroad. It is our "cross" experience.

After the death, resurrection and ascension of Jesus, the pattern was set. This was to be our course, as human consciousness would continue to evolve and mature over the next two thousand years. Now it is time to exit time itself, to step out of our mortality and be clothed with the light that perfection brings.

Jesus said something very interesting upon hearing that Herod wanted to have him killed:

> *Go tell that fox that I do cures today and tomorrow, and the third day I shall be perfected. (Luke 13:32)*

Many see this present millennium, the third millennium since his death and resurrection, as the *third day* that Jesus referenced. The reason many people believe this is because of what Peter says— when he equates one day as a thousand years:

> *But do not forget this one thing, dear friends: With the Lord a day is like a thousand years, and a thousand years are like a day. (2 Peter 3:8)*

Many believe the year 2000, the beginning of the third millennium, is marking the beginning of the "third day." So we see that Jesus set a pattern in scripture. Viewed historically he was crucified and resurrected on the third day but viewed metaphorically we see another pattern emerge. We are entering into the third day (the third millennium), just as in the pattern, Jesus resurrected from the dead on the (literal) third day we will do likewise in the third millennium as awakened and enlightened beings having overcome fear and death. This is the mystery of entering into eternal life, not gaining entrance to the kingdom of heaven only after we die, as most of Christian dogma espouses. The Divine seed penetrated humanity two thousand years ago and has been germinating, growing inside the consciousness of the human being, albeit sentenced to death in a mortal body. This Divine seed has experienced death and has been in the bowels of the earth for two millennia just as Jesus was in the underworld for two days before his resurrection and as in the archetype of Jonah inside the belly of the great fish for three days (more on Jonah later).

Jesus said, *"...the Kingdom is within you" (Luke 17:21)*

Jesus spoke this mystery alluding to the penetration of the Divine Spark into humanity. With Jesus among them they cast out demons, walked on water, healed the sick, cleansed the lepers and raised the dead. After his death, resurrection and ascension we see that life returned to normal among the disciples—supernatural acts subsided rapidly. So we see that in the time of Jesus even the shadows of the disciples healed the sick but upon the departure of Jesus years later, the disciple Timothy is sick and told by the Apostle Paul to drink wine to help with his ailments *(1 Timothy 5:3)*. Go figure. Jesus manifested another dimensional realm all around him. Jesus called Himself and the environment around him the *"bridegroom."* Let's take another look:

> *Then John's disciples came and asked him, "How is it that we and the Pharisees fast, but your disciples do not fast?" Jesus answered, "How can the guests of the bridegroom fast while he is with them? The time will come when the bridegroom will be taken from them; then they will fast. No one sews a patch of un-shrunk cloth on an old garment, for the patch will pull away from the garment, making the tear worse. Neither do men pour new wine into old wineskins. If they do, the skins will burst, the wine will run out and the wineskins will be ruined. No, they pour new wine into new wineskins, and both are preserved." (Matthew 9:14-17)*

The *"bridegroom"* is an environment of union expressed through Jesus where the ego has willfully submitted as a bride to a groom. Notice that Jesus did not call himself a "groom" or a "bride" but rather he used the word *"bridegroom."* When the ego willfully submits to the groom, another environment is produced, another dimensional level within the present age. Jesus manifested the realm of the kingdom all around him where even the disciples could work the miraculous. The "fast" in the natural represents the denial of sustenance for the body—in the same way the kingdom provided sustenance for all of them to maintain an immortal state of being; but the kingdom dimension was taken from them; it was this environmental sustenance that would be denied them and us over the next two thousand millennia. We have been fasting the sustenance of the supernatural realm.

We are now transitioning into the third day. Human consciousness has made the initial shift out of this passing age and into the age to come. We are in for one heck of a ride and need a new container for metaphorical/intuited understanding (wineskin) to contain the coming volatile and expanding consciousness. Those within fundamental religious structures will have to let go of some ideas, especially some concepts about Jesus and dogma that have severely limited their growth if they are to grasp these new (old) thoughts. Jesus has left the building

Summary Points:

- Fear will not support the expanding consciousness now on the planet.
- We must let go of fear-based mentalities to contain the new consciousness.
- We must be able to expand with new consciousness and contract—exhaling what no longer serves human kind.
- Those remaining in fear-based systems will reject those migrating out. Being ostracized is the order of the day for those transitioning in consciousness.
- There needs to be a restrictive womb-like environment to birth the Christ.

- You cannot circumvent another person's path. Each must unfold at their own pace.
- The age to come is not comprised of consensus.
- The ego is a servant of the Christ.
- Humanity stands at a crossroads where our humanity intersects our Divinity. It is our "cross" experience.

Chapter Five

Letting Jesus Go and Introducing Metaphoric Templates

Consciousness is a living, breathing organism of sorts that grows and evolves as humanity forges and navigates new frontiers in thought. The metaphorical application of the Bible is gaining popularity, letting go of what has previously been interpreted literally. This is not a new concept. Throughout the ages many brave souls have introduced this form of interpretation, some with great consequence. I hope this book is a catalyst that introduces a wonderful new perspective on an ancient book. To make the shift in consciousness requires a letting go of rigidly held interpretations. Jesus may not be who and what you think he is. Broadening your understanding of the teachings of Jesus will give you fresh insight into ancient teaching and rituals.

The Old Testament records humanity's journey while the immature and limited ego is in charge of consciousness and provides rules, regulations, boundaries *and* consequences, just like a parent disciplining a child. Conversely, the New Testament teachings of Jesus introduce existence outside the parental guidance of the law presented in the Old Testament, as consciousness matures out from egocentric domination and into its true identity as Divinity.

Jesus introduced liberty from the law and established a pattern to bring the life of egocentric domination willingly into a place of death. Paul provided oversight to this fledgling Divinity consciousness as it moved out from egocentric domination to fulfill the pattern revealed by the life of Jesus. Paul is a governor of sorts to this coming of age "teenager" that is seeking transition into adulthood. He gently led this tender consciousness out from the law by amplifying the teachings of Jesus and in some examples by pulling the mysterious metaphors out from literalism. Paul was given a difficult task indeed to help steer consciousness, sometimes with rules and regulations, as it vacillated back and forth between law and grace and between historical edicts and mystery. There are clearly two ages represented in the New Testament. One is the present age and one is the kingdom or the *age to come* as Jesus put it *(Luke 18:30)*. Generally speaking, Christianity fails to see this delineation and cherry-picks Old Testament restrictions to blend with New Testament grace and as such has produced a confused and contradictory religion.

Historically, Christianity under the Roman Empire kept most of the ancient mystery texts that reflect the metaphorical understanding of Christ's teaching secretly hidden away. They canonized those texts that were in keeping with their understanding at that time. Anything too mystical was kept out of the cannon. Likewise, the burning of the Library of Alexandria destroyed many of these important documents. Christianity has basically claimed exclusive rights to the Bible canonizing their selection of scripture and by interpreting it to suit their doctrines. Also, Christianity has absorbed many ideals and concepts from the intervention of Constantine around the time when the Council at Nicaea was held—a full three hundred years after the timeframe of Jesus Christ. Because of their exclusive claim on scripture, Christianity has earned a level of scorn. This claim in part, may be a catalyst for Atheism, a label for those who do not believe in the God that has been presented and defined by Christian fundamentalism. Atheism is an ever growing sector of consciousness that does not support or tolerate their intolerable God. If God is what Christianity represents, they want no part of it, and I don't blame them.

Fundamentalist dogma does not accurately reflect the Bible's pattern and intent for evolving consciousness. The Bible, however, void of the overlay of such dogma, presents evolving consciousness well. It is time to look beyond the constraints of religion, beyond the husk of the shell to find the pearls hidden within.

Nevertheless I tell you the truth; It is expedient for you that I go away: for if I go not away, the Comforter will not come

> *unto you; but if I depart, I will send him unto you. (John 16:7)*

In the scripture above, Jesus speaks as though there is an option as to whether or not we let him *go away*. I think we do have the option; do we cling to the ideal of this external Savior, the husk of the shell of the human, beaten and bloody, dead and resurrected or do we allow the historical figure to rest in peace? As a historical figure within Christianity, Jesus is worshipped as the Savior of mankind, the one and only Son of God. As the metaphorical figure, he is the *pearl of great price*, a pattern, the way for us to follow so that we too might tap into our limitless potential of the Christ within:

> *To them God has chosen to make known among the Gentiles the glorious riches of this mystery, which is Christ in you, the hope of glory. (Colossians 1:27)*

Do we worship the external ideal or do we embrace and understand what his life, death and resurrection stood for metaphorically? If we cling to the foot of the cross at Calvary, we miss the open grave. If we carry the image of a beaten and bloodied man on the cross, we miss the inference that we too must come to the place where our humanity intersects our Divinity and the life of self, as we know it, comes to an end. This life of self or ego loves to see the conflict that arises when it discerns something good or evil or greater or lesser than itself and flourishes in the midst of this duality. It flourishes because that is exactly what it was created to do—judge between good and evil. That is the ego's job. But now the Divine Spark within waits patiently for our conscious participation in the awakening process where duality gives way to singularity or union if you will. Our conscious participation includes following the teaching of Jesus that says, *"Judge not."*

The events recorded in the Bible are not there for history's sake; they are there to show you the "way" out from duality or eating from the tree of the knowledge of good and evil and into the abundant "life".

Understanding the need to let the historical account of Jesus go is paramount to our spiritual development. Letting the historical account go does not necessarily mean it did not actually happen. It means that we are open to see and embrace the metaphorical intent, *pattern* or *template*. Until now the ego needed to see this historical human pattern expressed outside of itself in the life and death of Jesus in order that someday it would begin to see the pattern and its internal application. This presents a real problem for fundamentalists as the fear of not believing in this historical savior gives one the title of "anti-christ" and sentences one to everlasting torment in hell. We are the only begotten, patterned by Jesus, that has been given to "save" the world but we must believe in who and what we are.

> *For God so loved the world that he gave his one and only Son, that whoever believes in him shall not perish but have eternal life. For God did not send his Son into the world to condemn the world, but to save the world through him. (John 3:16-17)*

We are a corporeal man.

Lest the entire message of Christ be in vain, we need to see the pattern that was set through the crucifixion, resurrection and ascension, for this is our story.

Within my fundamentalism I would arrogantly look down upon the Catholics for their worship of a dead Jesus on a cross. Idol worship I thought, along with Mary and all those dead saints. Didn't they see their error? However, it wasn't long before I realized I had been doing the same thing wearing the empty cross around my neck. Whether we worship the dead Jesus on the cross or the resurrected one, we miss the mark. Lest the entire message of Jesus Christ be in vain, we need to see the pattern that was set through the crucifixion, resurrection and ascension, for this is our story. We are to walk this same path in consciousness. Jesus said this:

> *Whosoever therefore shall confess me before men, him will I confess also before my Father which is in heaven. But whosoever shall deny me before men, him will I also deny before my Father which is in heaven. (Matthew 10:32-33)*

Fundamentalism uses this scripture as evidence for their dogma that says you have to raise your hand to accept Jesus into your heart in front of the congregation or at the very least you must tell someone that you have done it. I supported this practice for many decades and now that I see scripture in lieu of an internal Christ being formed within. I see things differently, so differently that I am told that I am deceived. To deny Christ is to not become what he patterned for us. When Jesus says he will deny us before the Father if we deny him, means that until we believe who and what we are and the ego becomes subservient to Divinity, we will be denied access to this most potent creative potential that lies within us. This endowment is for the bride alone.

> *Dear friends, now we are children of God, and what we will be has not yet been made known. But we know that when Christ appears, we shall be like him, for we shall see him as he is. (1 John 3:2)*

To deny Christ is to deny his presence and existence within us as the Christ. Paul said he labored and travailed until Christ is formed in us:

> *My little children, of whom I travail in birth again until Christ be formed in you. (Galatians 4:19)*

It is this confession that is not being made. Christians in general are afraid of saying anything like it. *But Christ is not Jesus.* Christ is a title given to anyone who is spiritually enlightened and understands the journey of Divinity into humanity; accepting the command to judge not and to love one another. This precious root of Divinity is growing in the midst of the soil of the earth, in us, uncomely humanity. Awakening Divinity has come to ransom *itself.* We must come to the point of recognizing that Christ (egoless consciousness) must be made Lord of the body, claiming for itself its much-anticipated helpmate that has been under construction for millennia.

There is a scripture that springs to mind, one that Christians feel tells us to worship Jesus:

> *So that at the name of Jesus every knee will bow, of those who are in heaven and on earth and under the earth and*

every tongue confess that Jesus Christ is Lord, to the glory of God the Father. (Philippians 2:10-11)

It says, *"...every knee will bow and every tongue confesses that Jesus Christ is Lord."* My knee (ego-centric nature) bows to the Christ within and that Christ is now the "Lord" of my body. This is an act of an ego in submission to the Christ within. Jesus the man manifested this belief and understanding of who it was that indwelled him—the Father, the creative component within us all. Jesus exists historically as a pattern *and* as the firstborn of many brothers - brothers of flesh and blood, couched in humanity and destined to experience resurrection. Externally viewed, it presents a deity that is worshipped errantly like the account of the serpent on the pole *(Numbers 21)*. Internally it presents Christ in you, you becoming what you behold.

It is vital to see our purpose as Divinity immersed into humanity to experience duality.

Many will look at the scripture I cited earlier about Jesus going away and say that it was a precursor to the death, resurrection, and ascension. And historically, it is. I also choose, however, to see it metaphorically, letting the historical account of Jesus go so that I might embrace the mystery. We, as sentient beings are born into the manger of humanity, growing up within the biology of mortality, awakening to our true identity as Divinity, willingly bringing the ego to death and resurrecting the same as a servant. Within this beautiful story we see the human becoming the helpmate of the Divine so that the immaterial essence of the Divine has the framework of a material body to inhabit, explore, and create worlds of matter. That's a mouthful.

If you are willing to see certain Biblical events as prophetic and metaphoric, I have a great example to share with you. I call these events "templates" because within the history we can see the mystery of our own journey in human consciousness. It is vital to see our purpose as Divinity immersed into humanity to experience duality. I will introduce this concept over several chapters so stay with me. You may have to read the metaphoric interpretation a few times so be patient. In doing so, that bridge we discussed in Chapter Three is being built within your consciousness.

First, let me reinforce the application of literalism and metaphor as it pertains to the interpretation of scripture:

Literal translation: Historical and external (outside of ourselves) application.

Metaphorical translation: Mystical and possibly internal (inside of ourselves) application.

I'll give you an example to help you understand what I mean by leaving the history for the mystery. Let's view a very well known (external/historical) event in the Old Testament and see if it has internal/mystical/metaphorical application. We will look at the historical application first.

Historical account of Moses and the Red Sea

The Israelites journeyed out of their land to seek refuge and to be spared from four hundred years of prophesied drought. They travelled to Egypt, where they flourished. Nearly four hundred years pass and Pharaoh fearing their growing numbers and influence enslaved them and issued an edict to kill all male children born to them. To prevent his death, two Israelites laid their son, Moses, in a basket lined with pitch so that it would float down the Nile River. It was found, and Pharaoh's daughter raised the infant. It was in this environment that Moses grew to be a young man. Once an adult, he realized who he was. He was given the charge by God to free his kin, the Israelites, from slavery and to tell the taskmaster Pharaoh to *"Let my people go."* After resisting this decree, Pharaoh and Egypt received the wrath of God via ten horrible plagues, the last of which was death to the firstborn males in Egypt that ultimately took the life of Pharaoh's firstborn son. The Israelites were instructed to place the blood of a slaughtered lamb on their doorposts so that when the angel of death came to kill the firstborn sons, it would pass by those homes with blood on the door portal. Upon the death of his firstborn son, Pharaoh finally relented and released the Israelites to return home, but soon changed his mind and pursued them to the brink of the Red Sea. Moses touched his staff to the waters and they parted, leaving a path of dry land for them to cross over. With the Israelites safely on the other side, the armies of Pharaoh, with horses and chariots, began the trek through the parted Red Sea, only to be drowned when the walls of water collapsed around them. The Israelites wandered in the wilderness forty years, were bitten by venomous serpents and many died there. Only the new generation, born in the wilderness, who were never in bondage to Egypt, made it into the Promised Land, with two exceptions: Joshua and Caleb.

Now let's look at a metaphorical application subjectively:

Metaphorical account of Moses and the Red Sea

Egypt and Pharaoh represent an environment dominated by the "taskmaster" of our own internal ego-driven life. We see that the whole nation of Israel (representing Divinity within all humankind) must leave their homeland (spiritual wholeness) and enter into slavery and egocentric bondage in Egypt, a necessary experience for the collective whole as it leaves its immortal status and continually eats from the tree of the knowledge of good and evil that produces duality and mortality.

Moses, an archetype of a deliverer, while immersed in humanity (during a time where the male children are being slaughtered) was given to another mother to be raised. This is a metaphor of our deliverer, the ego that yields to Divinity within man, given over to an egocentric (fear-based) environment in which to grow and learn and to eventually overcome it, just as Jesus modeled for us. Moses lived to be 120 years old, a number that represents the limit one may live as a mortal (Genesis 6:3).

Moses was hidden in symbolic baseness, a straw basket (limited humanity), floating down the Nile (water = human consciousness) and was found by Pharaoh's daughter (egocentric environment) who raised him. Entering adulthood, Moses awakened to the knowledge that he would serve as a deliverer of his people and lead them out of slavery to Egypt. Metaphorically, this is what occurs within the human being when it consciously awakens and realizes its true identity as a partner to Divinity and its task to overcome egocentric domination (slavery to ego). We are all charged with being the savior of our body and to seize the promised land of immortality.

Pharaoh/Egypt (the egocentric domination) was reluctant to release Moses and the slaves (Divinity imbued humanity held captive by the ego) and subsequently received many plagues as a result of this stubborn determination. The plagues all represent various conditions of humanity (sickness, dis-ease, baseness, etc.) as it remains in an egocentric state of consciousness.

The last plague was death of the firstborn son (this firstborn son is representative of our mortal condition brought about by the egocentric domination). The firstborn represents our condition as being born first as a human (secondly as Divinity awakening within humanity). In other words, the symbolism of Passover is that the firstborn, our mortal flesh and blood, *does not have to die.*

The slaves were instructed to place the blood of a slaughtered lamb (Christ consciousness; gentle as a lamb; the Christ being delivered up to death; we willingly bring our egocentric life into death to experience union with the Divine) on the doorpost so that when the angel of death passed by, the firstborn would be spared. This is called the Passover. Pharaoh did no such thing and his firstborn died, and in his grief, he relented and let the slaves go free.

The blood on the doorpost (portal) is a metaphor for the act of union when the virginal hymen breaks and blood is shed and coats the portal—the union between Divinity and man, the bride and groom etc. The portal here represents the Vessica Pisces, a symbol of the birth portal or metaphoric and/or cosmic vagina and also representing the Age of Pisces where the Christ seed would penetrate the human frame.

Therefore, metaphorically we can see that in this union in consciousness with the Divine, the slain lamb (the human in willful submission to Divinity) is essential for mankind to be released from egocentric domination. As the Israelites headed for the Promised Land, Pharaoh's armies chased them to the brink of the Red Sea (human consciousness). While leading the slaves, Moses used his staff to touch the water, thereby parting it so that they could pass over to the other side. As Pharaoh's armies chased them, the Israelites arrived safely on the other side, and the waters of the parted Red Sea collapsed in on the Egyptians. This account of the parted Red Sea is a perfect metaphor for man's dual and divided consciousness, eating from the tree of the knowledge of good and evil. Reality is formed with his thinking of separateness, replete with the strength of Pharaoh's horses and chariots (the ego's strength and tactics), buried within the waters of consciousness of the human mind—an unstable condition that would follow them into the wilderness.

The story continues as the Israelites wander in the wilderness, as it reflects our own journey and struggle to recognize the influence, domination and control of the human ego within our consciousness. The former slaves wandering in the wilderness were being bitten by "serpents" (symbolic of egocentric consciousness and choices) and dying. The tribe needed to find a cure, and so the image of a serpent raised on a pole (the crucified ego and subsequent resurrecting of that transformed nature) was given to them by God and they were told to build it and to *"look to it."* Upon looking to it, they are told they would receive their healing. (This symbol is more commonly known as the Caduceus, the symbol of healing in the medical field).

Next the wanderers began to worship the image rather than look to it. Isn't this what we have done with Jesus? Rather than to understand the mystical application of this historical advent and to embrace the pattern, *we worship the image*. If we could only peer through this mystical lens we would see what a beautiful picture this serpent on the pole is of our own rising consciousness. Death of this "self" on the pole serves as a metaphor as we experience egocentric death and spiritual rebirth as the ego yields to our Divinity. Energy ascends the spinal column in a serpentine fashion as consciousness moves from fear into love. This is the crucifixion process where our Divinity intersects our humanity. As it was, their idolatrous worship of the image caused God to issue an edict to destroy the serpent and the pole. Metaphorically speaking, when we fail to discern the pattern by worshipping the image rather than looking *to* the image we have a death sentence that looms over us—and are we subject to disease, decay and death? Yes, we are mortal while we remain egocentric.

Such profound truth can be found if we are willing to forsake the history and enter into the mystery of spiritual texts. Jesus was and is a mystic. We would be wise to see his teachings through a mystical lens. The key to shifting in consciousness is in understanding the mystical interpretation of historical scriptural texts. This will change everything we know about spirituality.

Metaphorical Key:

Slaves: All of mortal mankind temporarily and purposely subjected to ego.

Pharaoh: Egocentric environment that the human is given over to, purposely, in order to be "saved" from the death of the firstborn—the edict issued by ego to prevent the deliverer or "Christ" from growing within the ranks of humanity.

Egypt: The domain or kingdom of the ego within all.

Basket Lined with Pitch: The container of base humanity, limited biology, our firstborn condition as mortals, navigating within human consciousness (water, the river Nile).

Pharaoh's Daughter: Egocentric, temporary guardian of the mortal.

Plagues: The many afflictions of mortality that we will experience if ego does not relinquish its grip on humanity.

Lamb: Man's divine nature that demonstrates pure non-resistance and allows the death of egocentric nature by yielding to Divinity (a lamb will stand perfectly still when slaughtered).

Lamb's Blood: The price of union "shedding blood", the price of egocentric death to mortal self-life.

Doorpost: The portal where union between mortal (ego) and immortal (Divinity) culminates. This is within man's consciousness, where the Christ is born. The blood metaphorically represents the broken virginal hymen in the consciousness of the human as it submits to union.

Firstborn/Death of the Firstborn: We are first born of flesh and blood and are mortal beings, and secondly of Spirit or Divinity. Thus the firstborn is our mortality and this is what dies when there has not been "union", or when ego does not willingly give way to Divinity, so that the conception of the Christ nature may begin (the last of the plagues, death of the firstborn is the mortal lifespan or limitation of 120 years of life according to Genesis 6:3).

The Reticent Release of Israel: The ego finally releases the human from domination because of sorrow and despair.

The Water or the Red Sea: Water symbolizes the consciousness of man.

Divided Red Sea: Duality consciousness, judging good from evil.

The Staff of Moses: The consciousness of humanity in an awakened state, the spinal column with the Djed (light) having risen on the spine (serpent/kundalini energy on the pole), so that when it touches the Red Sea the consciousness parts, and humanity is allowed to journey temporarily with Divine providence through duality.

The Horses and Chariots of Pharaoh Buried in the Red Sea: The strength of the ego (horses and chariots from Egypt) is buried within the consciousness of mankind (water) a condition that would follow them into the wilderness and as they enter into the Promised Land (immortality) to continue their journey in apprehending Christ consciousness.

Serpents in the Wilderness: Egocentric nature that keeps striking mankind in a mortal state, inoculating him, insuring mortality.

The Ascending Serpent on the Pole: The successful migration of egocentric consciousness undergoing transformation from lowest (fear) to Christ consciousness (love) as our conscious energy ascends through our chakra system to the top of our spinal column (the pole).

"Look" to the Serpent on the Pole: Understanding the pattern in, and the journey through, duality to bring about ultimate healing, the state of immortality.

Worshipping the Pole: Thinking and believing that healing comes from an external worship of an idol or entity and failing to see our own Divinity within.

Destruction of the Serpent on the Pole: The dismantling and ultimate demise of Christianity as a relevant religion and the recognition of ego worship as idolatrous.

The Son of Man is humanity expressed through slumbering Divinity ~ The Son of God is Divinity expressed through awakened humanity.

The imagery found within this example is so pregnant with metaphorical meaning. Here we begin to see the nature of the Son of Man (ego-led) and the Son of God (Spirit-led) defined.

The Son of Man is humanity expressed through slumbering Divinity—The Son of God is Divinity expressed through awakened humanity. The key to ascension and resurrection is in understanding the fundamental difference between the ego and Divine self or the Son of Man and the Son of God.

Once you begin to see the metaphorical value of scripture it is hard to see it any other way. This wonderful book has been intended for today's awakening masses to give us information, inspiration, hope and a plan.

Summary Points:

- Consciousness is a living-breathing organism of sorts that grows and evolves as humanity continually forges new frontiers in thought.
- Fundamentalism may be a catalyst for Atheism.
- We must let the historical Jesus "go."

- The crucifixion, resurrection and ascension are our story. We are to walk the same path in consciousness.
- The human is the helpmate of the Divine.
- Divinity immersed itself into humanity to experience duality.
- Literalism allows for the egocentric consciousness of the human to learn historical events.
- Metaphoric or mystical interpretation allows for our intuitive ability to surface seeing historical and external events as internal and mystical.
- The Son of Man is humanity expressed through slumbering Divinity—The Son of God is Divinity expressed through awakened humanity. The key to ascension and resurrection is in understanding the fundamental difference between the ego and Divine self or the Son of Man and the Son of God.

Chapter Six

Christ is a Verb—Come in the Flesh

For years I had a general discomfort about Christianity and, like many, I found it difficult to separate the fundamentalist religion from Jesus. I have known so many wonderful, caring and genuine people within the system of Christianity and I thought that they must know something I didn't. However, the systematic approach to God that fundamentalism employs became unsettling to me and my discomfort grew daily it seemed. I was told what to believe about the devil, Jesus, God, heaven and hell all of my life and had done very little to challenge the information. Oftentimes when I would hear concepts about a punitive God it would not sit well with me. Instead of investigating for myself I would reluctantly accept or acquiesce because everyone else did. After all, I wanted to be right and those around me seemed to think it so.

I had been out of the church system for roughly four years when the following happened; I had been out shopping and was re-entering my neighborhood driving by the familiar Catholic Church on the corner and I had this thought run across my mind:

What if Christianity has it ALL wrong?

The thought hit me like a thunderbolt. I was disturbed and fascinated both at the same time. Then came this question:

Is it wrong to worship Jesus?

Where did that thought come from? I was perplexed. Then I wondered, *did Jesus ever ask or command to be worshipped?* That began many months of questioning and searching, not just scripture but I began to sift through the many teachings I had received over the years and question the various doctrines I had embraced. I felt that I needed to let go of any dogma that I knew had no basis in scripture and more than that, things that didn't *resonate within me* as true. I was overcome with way too much information and I thought, there has got to be an easier way to find the truth.

I could not get the scripture out of my mind about letting Jesus go:

> *Nevertheless I tell you the truth; it is expedient for you that I go away: for if I go not away, the Comforter will not come unto you; but if I depart, I will send him unto you. (John 16:7)*

Finally, after weeks of trepidation and struggle, in a prayer-like way I prayed to Jesus and said, *"Okay—I am letting you go. I am letting it all go."*

I imagined all of my pet doctrines and beliefs listed on a huge blackboard and a giant eraser rubbing it all away into nothingness. In silence and in a matter of moments, I let go of my beliefs about heaven, hell, the rapture and the devil, and my precious Lord Jesus; all ideas involving some of the main tenets of my faith. By letting the Christian idea of Jesus go, something marvelous happened; fear left me. I had spent most of my life living in fear and suddenly it was gone. It was no longer important for me to think or reason according to a set of religious principles outlined by someone else. I began to trust my instincts. Something other than my intellect was now guiding me, speaking to me, bringing comfort and peace. And it was wonderful!

By letting the Christian idea of Jesus go, something marvelous happened; fear left me.

Letting the Christian idea of Jesus "go", meant that I had made the choice to embrace his life and teachings differently than how a religious system told me to think and believe. I could now look at things metaphorically rather than literally if I wanted to. I made the conscious choice to think and discern for myself about who this Jesus was, and what he would mean to me from that day forward. It was my day of liberation. I would never return to the confinement of fundamentalism and literalism; I had become fearless and felt comfortable for the first time in my spiritual exodus from organized religion. I was born *again*.

The term "born again" is more accurately translated, born from above. To be born from above means to be borne out from human-hood and into Divinity; it is a perspective change. I was beginning to perceive spiritual principles outside and above limited human reasoning and consciousness. Without fear of deception, hell, death and separation there was no restriction in my thinking. I was free to learn and explore whatever captured my heart's interest. I was now looking into forbidden books like the Kabbalah, *A Course in Miracles*, and even things written by Edgar Cayce and other channeled material. In Christianity receiving information from a higher source outside of you is called prophesy—but outside of Christianity, it is called channeling and many fundamentalists consider it witchcraft or sorcery. Back then, I had been curious about this non-Christian material and had purchased some of it. Then I was told that they were of the devil and the occult and that I needed to burn them. Do you know how much charcoal starter it takes to burn a Kabbalah?

Once I had let the historical figure go, it became important to me to understand the word that follows the name Jesus and that is "Christ." When someone says the word Christ, people automatically think of Jesus. Some think it is actually a surname of sorts for Him. I have heard it said that the word "Christ" was around centuries before the advent of Jesus and was used to describe a person who understood the mysteries and was considered an "initiate" into mysticism and *anointed* with special understanding.

The word Christ should be considered a verb, because it expresses *a mode of being*. The word Christ actually means anoint, to *rub* or to *press into* and is not exclusive to Jesus. So what was rubbed or pressed into Jesus? And if Jesus is a pattern for us, then how are we likewise to be *anointed*? Christ is not a term limited to one single person; it is a term for anyone who experiences "anointing" or enlightenment. The scripture says that this Christ is, or will be in us; *(Colossians 1:27)* For clarification, that is not a little

Jesus somewhere nestled within our heart after we recite the sinner's prayer or accept him as our personal Lord and Savior.

Let's take a good look at what anointing is literally and metaphorically, and the place that this Christedness should have in our lives. To worship is to emulate, not to project emotion toward something outside of us, although the Old Testament (old consciousness) pattern shows this. But Jesus sought to show them an inverted reality; that is, Divinity dwells within the temple made without hands, the human being.

My husband and I were in Maui, Hawaii on business several years ago and had taken some time out for shopping. We were in a funky little gift store just off of the beach where they sold souvenirs. I happened upon a t-shirt that showed a picture of Jesus beautifully robed and smiling with his arms stretched open and standing behind a sofa. The caption read: *"I found Jesus...He was behind the couch."* At first I snickered and quickly walked away thinking it was a bit irreverent. I returned a minute later again standing in front of it, smiling and thinking, *it is wonderfully irreverent*. Again, walking through the store I was unable to contain my growing laughter and returned to the shirt and was now laughing out loud. I purchased the shirt that day and gave it to my oldest son, Ryan. He has a great sense of humor and I knew he would appreciate it. Fundamentalism does no favors for Jesus when he is presented as a hiding himself and can only be found through *them*. And most often is found in a church that pressures members for tithes and offerings to pay for the building and salaries of its employees. We do need to search but our search should not extend *outside of ourselves*. The Old Testament book of the Song of Solomon gives light to this romance that if taken metaphorically is found within in the inner rooms of the heart.

The basis for the word Christ then, is when Divinity and flesh meet in conscious awareness.

As I journeyed further away from the literal interpretation of scripture I saw a pattern or template emerge from the Old Testament account of Esther that brought me further understanding of the word Christ. In the book, Esther was being prepared to meet the King to become his Queen and as such she was having her skin anointed with perfumed oil. Oil is a perfect metaphor for Spirit or Divinity. Once oil is rubbed into the skin, the oil is irretrievable as the skin and the oil have become one. The oil is now animated as it mingles with flesh and the flesh becomes supple and beautiful. It is a mutually beneficial relationship. Metaphorically we can see that the oil or Divinity (Spirit) and the flesh (metaphor for baseness) become ONE—like a marriage.

The story of Esther is metaphoric for our own process of anointing as we are prepared to meet the *king*. The basis for the word Christ then, is when Divinity and flesh meet in conscious awareness. Flesh is anointed as we awaken to the reality that Divinity indwells us. Divinity is *"pressed into"* the mortal framework and there are now two conscious elements dwelling in one body—*and the two become ONE.* Jesus was called "Emanuel" or God with man. This meeting is a culmination of a courtship between Divinity and human consciousness that has lasted millennia.

As the story continues, Esther presents herself before the King and plans to ask for the salvation of her people who were under threat of imminent death at the hangman's gallows. We must ask ourselves, are we mortal and subject to imminent death? Are we petitioning for salvation? The King welcomes her into his presence and tells her to ask for anything, *anything* up to half of his kingdom. Wow—now that is a partnership. Her people were ultimately spared. And that is what comes with the anointing and is what happens to us as this Spark of Divinity expands or grows and becomes one with us. It is like the parable of the mustard seed planted in the Garden. It begins as the smallest of seeds but soon overtakes the "garden." It is perfection blossoming in and through us. This account of Esther and the King is a beautiful metaphor—the Queen (the womb of the egocentric human) comes boldly to her counterpart, the King (life giving seed giver, Spirit/Divinity) and is petitioning for the salvation of her people (the human race). The scriptures are indeed a roadmap for us, which if viewed metaphorically, reveal humanity's path through consciousness. And what a journey it is.

Many people within Christianity have been slammed down and pummeled into thinking that they are no good sinners, saved from a punishing God if they just accept Jesus into their heart and would stop sinning. And for God's sake, they should get into a church to pay their tithes and fellowship with others that believe the same as they do. They are told that there is no way that they could ever be good enough, but if Jesus lives in their heart they will pass the salvation test, escape everlasting torment in hell and be permitted to enter into heaven when they die. But, if we will never be good enough then why did Jesus say this?

Be perfect therefore, even as your heavenly Father is perfect. (Matthew 5:48)

Perfecting comes when union takes place. The Queen is now an equal partner with the King—and he offers her up to half of his kingdom. I don't think Jesus would have told us to be perfect if it were not possible. I know now that we too, are perfection in process. We are encouraged to believe in "Christ." It becomes necessary to stop seeing this Christ as external and historical and realize that Christ is an internal mode of being that is not exclusive to one person or to a small sector of humanity. Christ or *anointing* is when the human being awakens to the understanding that it is indwelt by a heretofore silent partner; this partner awaits the conscious choice of the human ego to yield to it as a bride to a groom, in the consummation of marriage or union. Christ is all, in all. Interestingly, the word consummate means *perfection*.

Here there is no Gentile or Jew, circumcised or uncircumcised, barbarian, Scythian, slave or free, but Christ is all, and is in all. (Colossians 3:11)

We must believe in "Christ" and that is not the Jesus that Christianity presents to us. Christ means that Divinity has been pressed into us and has been cohabiting with us in one body and most importantly, we have become conscious of it. This Christ will overcome the mortal realm and bring the body to a position of immortality. This is what it means to be saved and simply stated is the plan for humanity. Divinity is after a physical body as a helpmate so that it may find expression in the physical, material worlds—and that body is you.

We are here to discover the latent Spark of Divinity that lies dormant within us, the pearl within the oyster. This Christ is being formed in us, as us. As Christ is formed we begin to see the limitation and futility of life under egocentric domination and ultimately surrender. It is at the place of willful death to our egocentric, fear-centered self that resurrection takes place and our body becomes a habitation for the fullness of indwelling Divinity. And the human is anointed. This is the pattern of Jesus—death to self, burial, resurrection and ultimately ascension.

It is time to surrender the limitation of our dogma and run in search of the truth that Jesus' mysterious teachings provide. It is time to move from the restrictiveness of literalism and into the expansive halls of our intuitive abilities to dissect the metaphoric value in all scripture. Moreover, this is a time for all of humanity to abandon its prejudices and seek these valuable messages and discern for themselves. Humanity needs a wakeup call, especially those within fundamentalism. I speak from forty-three years of experience within the system and twelve years outside of it. I have experienced firsthand the ramifications that come from challenging traditional doctrine and thought and the vitriol that protects dogmatically held beliefs. Challenge yourself!

I read an article that quoted research done by former Evangelical Christine Wicker. The article stated, *"When asked to rate eleven groups in terms of respect, non-Christians rated evangelicals tenth. Only prostitutes ranked lower."* Ouch.

The article quotes Wicker further to say,

> *"Misbehavior is so widespread among evangelicals that one evangelical author (Ronald Sider) calls the statistics devastating. When pollster George Barna, himself an evangelical, looked at seventy moral behaviors, he didn't find any difference between the actions of those who were born-again Christians and those who weren't. His studies and other indicators show that divorce among born-agains is as common as, or more common than, among other*

groups. One study showed that wives in traditional, male-dominated marriages were 300 percent more likely to be beaten than wives in egalitarian marriages. Evangelicals make up only seven percent of the population, but about twenty percent of the women who get abortions. That information is staggering."

Wicker also states the declining consensus of Evangelical Christianity:

"Evangelical Christianity in America—supposedly Christianity's cutting edge—is dying. The facts are that about six thousand evangelicals walk away from their churches every day and most don't come back."

What is it that is turning so many people away from Christianity? In large part the judgment displayed through the dogma of elitism and intolerance has contributed to making fundamentalism unpalatable. Take it from me, I was one of them. I feel I have earned the right to be hardest on my tribe. I beat and thumped the Bible on many a head, controlled and manipulated consciousness through the use of fear-based theology. For some, dogma is learned quite young; like me having been programmed from adolescence. Being indoctrinated at a young age one must fight for the return of their intellectual property rights. Coming off of fundamentalism is like coming off of bad medicine; while you may think it cures your ills, it is ultimately addicting with church leaders and parishioners offering their dope of dogma to anyone who will make themselves subject to fear.

I realize these words may seem harsh for some and not harsh enough for others. That statement will most likely offend those still within the system. Some of those who have escaped fundamentalism know exactly what I am talking about. My goal is not to offend but to bring light on this "system" that claims it has the only pass into *heaven*. No, the Bible is not a Christian book and never was. Jesus did not come to start the Christian religion. Christian churches are built on Pagan sites and have adopted Pagan rituals from altars to robes and yet Christianity claims that Pagans are evil. It seems to me that the finger that points toward others in judgment now has to give an account for itself. They are not defenders of the faith because their faith is not identifiable with its namesake. Take a good hard look—Christian fundamentalism is a mess. This system of belief has become too small, too restrictive for today's blossoming consciousness. It is in need of the new wineskin that Jesus spoke of.

I talked to a close friend a few years back when faced with the possibility that Christianity just may be wrong about a few key beliefs and doctrines. He replied, *"I am too old to change the way that I think and I have no interest in learning anything new."* This is not uncommon for many Christians. They are indoctrinated and inoculated with fear and even when the truth as they know it is compromised, they resort to cognitive dissonance.

Cognitive dissonance is defined by Miriam Webster's as: *Mental conflict that occurs when beliefs or assumptions are contradicted by new information; when confronted with challenging new information, most people seek to preserve their current understanding of the world by rejecting, explaining away, or avoiding the new information or by convincing themselves that no conflict really exists.*

Here is a great quote from Franz Fanon regarding Cognitive Dissonance:

> *"Sometimes people hold a core belief that is very strong. When they are presented with evidence that works against that belief, the new evidence cannot be accepted. It would create a feeling that is extremely uncomfortable, called, cognitive dissonance. And because it is so important to protect the core belief, they will rationalize, ignore and even deny anything that doesn't fit in with the core belief."*

It takes a lot of fear and programming to hold onto dogma. When challenged, defenses are automatically raised to protect beliefs. When someone feels his or her beliefs are threatened, the brain releases the neurotransmitter norepinephrine. Norepinephrine is the same chemical that is released into the blood stream to aid in our survival when faced with danger. The *fight or flight* mechanism takes over making it impossible to accept or even to understand new information when it is presented. While the brain is under the influence of this chemical *it must defend itself.* This defensive posturing alienates fundamentalists because of the overarching belief that says they are the only ones that have it all "right."

I have recently shared a new spin on an old joke: *A Hindu dies and passes into eternity stopping at the pearly gates to speak with St. Peter. St. Peter tells him, "Go on in. You have full run of the place. Just don't go into the last room on the left." The Hindu asks, "Why may I not enter the last room on the left?" St. Peter replies, "Oh, that is where the Christians are and they think they are the only ones here."*

Christian fundamentalism is cultish at its core and this problem exists in many world religions, not just Christianity. But for those who distain Christianity I encourage you to look again at these mysterious teachings of Jesus. Don't judge him by what another person presents him to be.

> *I am the way, the truth and the life and no one comes to the Father but by me. (John 14:6)*

Fundamentalist Christianity asserts that one must get "saved" and submit to the church's idea of salvation. Now more than ever, we need to understand what Jesus meant when he said, *"no one comes to the Father but by me."* The *"by me"* is what needs clarification because there is great latitude taken by fundamentalism as to what this means. Does it mean that you must raise a hand, walk an aisle and accept Jesus into your heart? If yes, then why did Jesus never give instructions to do that? Each person needs to discern for him or herself what this "way" means and not let a fear-based religion interpret for them. Many believe in this limited idea of salvation and what it means to be "saved" because they have been programmed to do so. This idea and other erroneous doctrines are eventually acquiesced into the mass Christian consciousness through repetition.

I believe the life of Jesus modeled a path of transcendence through and out of egocentric humanity and into our core identity, Divinity. This is the "way" that he walked. Albert Einstein said,

"The intuitive mind is a sacred gift and the rational mind is a faithful servant. We have created a society that honors the servant and has forgotten the gift."

Jesus came to remind us, to show us the way back to the sacred gift. The servant is our egocentric intellect and its mode of operation is fear while it flourishes in fear-based systems. The gift is the intuitive mind and it is fearless. This is where Divinity flourishes.

The revolutionary life of Jesus taught us to Love God and to love our neighbor as ourselves. He brought his life of self and ego willingly into a place of crucifixion and ultimately resurrection. This may have happened in the physical to Jesus but it is said that he *died for us* so that our sins (life of egocentric domination) would be pardoned. In other words, we don't have to experience physical crucifixion via physical mortal death, but rather figurative crucifixion. Jesus is a pattern for all of humanity. This is the WAY, the TRUTH and the LIFE. He came to model a path out from fear and fear-based systems and to reveal the Father within us all. This is not a Christian Father, or a Jewish Father, it is pure, Divine, and creative potential, unveiled so that we might have abundant and eternal life. The Father is *the* primogenitor, the beginning of all eternal and immortal life, and it dwells within us. It is a life giving source, the Garden of Eden, a wellspring whose way is guarded while the human is egocentric. The way of self-LESS-ness that Jesus patterned for us is the only way to tap into this source. No one comes to this source unless they follow the way of the cross and willingly surrender the life of self to death so that in resurrection, a divine servant manifests.

The message we learn from Jesus dying on a cross and resurrecting is not unlike the many other cultural and mythological stories expressed in and through the lives of many masters. It is the hero's journey and is not exclusive to Christianity. Many diverse cultural icons have stories and lives that parallel the life of Jesus; most of them pre-date Jesus, complete with a supernatural birth, death and resurrection. The story is even told in our constellations. Unfortunately when fundamentalists are confronted with this knowledge they dismiss these other cultural icons as counterfeits, *masquerading as angels of light (2 Corinthians 11:14).* These masquerading angels of light however, are none other than the egocentric human being.

But the truth of who and what we are, is everywhere with nature itself testifying to us, of the wonder of it all.

Jesus tells us that the Father dwells within us so why do fundamentalists judge someone else's spiritual journey and hold the threat of hell, damnation and separation over them?

Do not judge, or you too will be judged. For in the same way you judge others, you will be judged, and with the measure you use, it will be measured to you. (Matthew 7:1)

Jesus clearly held a difference in perception between the tyrant Jehovah of the Old Testament and his father. They are *not* one and the same. The Old Testament deity is presented externally as one whose presence dwelled in a box (the Ark of the Covenant) and who expressed ego-driven and human characteristics (Jehovah was jealous, condemning, violent, intolerant, judgmental, murderous just like us.) And the other, the Father, we are told by Jesus, is within (the metaphoric Ark of the Covenant, the human heart). To follow Jesus requires a heart change—out from egocentric habits and patterns of selfishness and into love. That's it. This is where the Father resides—it is love—it is highly creative energy and Jesus patterned and charted the course to find this most powerful and creative source—within. Old Testament imagery provides a glimpse into what is seen within, our own internal workings under the law, therefore we have a God like Jehovah. The New Testament offers to us an alternative view if we are willing to see it—a journey out from the tyranny of the ego and into our identity as Divinity. Both Old and New Testaments may be seen as allegorical, displaying our human journey in consciousness. This inversion of the types and shadows found in scripture will help us see and to understand the stories of the unfolding and evolving human becoming a god-man—the Emanuel—the savior of the world.

Summary Points:

- It is absolutely necessary to separate Jesus from Christianity— this is "letting Jesus go" or letting go of what you have been taught by another and learn for yourself.
- Exiting literalism equals liberation.
- It takes a lot of charcoal starter to burn a Kabbalah.
- Born again means to be borne out from your human-hood and into your Divinity.
- Without fear there is no restriction in consciousness.
- The terms "Christ" and "Christian" were around centuries before the advent of Jesus.
- To worship is to emulate (to match or surpass) or to become— not to project emotion or allegiance toward something outside of ourselves... necessarily.
- "Christ" expresses a mode of being (a verb).
- The basis for the word Christ is when Divinity and flesh meet.
- Perfecting comes when union takes place.
- This Christ is being formed in us, as us.
- It is time to move from the restrictiveness of literalism and into the expansive halls of our intuitive abilities.
- Christianity loses six thousand members a day.
- Jesus did not come to start the Christian religion.
- It takes a lot of fear to reinforce Christian dogma.
- The life of Jesus modeled a path of transcendence through egocentric humanity and into our Divinity, our core identity.
- Albert Einstein said, *"The intuitive mind is a sacred gift and the rational mind is a faithful servant. We have created a society that honors the servant and has forgotten the gift."*
- Erroneous information about God and Jesus is acquiesced into our mass consciousness through repetition.
- Jesus came to model a path out from fear and fear-based systems and to reveal the Father within us all. This is not a Christian Father or a Jewish Father, it is pure Divinity.

- To follow Jesus requires a heart change—out from egocentric habits and patterns of selfishness and into love.

Phase Three

Understanding the Templates

Chapter Seven

You are the Virgin Mary

The word "seed" carries with it remarkable symbolism. Jesus used the word "seed" many times as he sought to relay a powerful image and to reveal the process of Divinity's investment into humanity, into the garden of man's consciousness. This germination and growth process has spanned millennia and is now reaching its coming of age. This Divine consciousness that has been embedded into the human being uses intuition to aid in its interpretation of reality; it utilizes symbolism and metaphor, by-passing limited human reasoning and employing it as a servant only when necessary. As mentioned in Chapter One, the intuitive mind is activated and comes as a *"thief in the night"* to apprehend spiritual truths in unfolding human consciousness by doing away with literalism. "Night" represents our darkened consciousness. This "Christ" consciousness appears suddenly and becomes the premiere operating system within our human consciousness. Once activated, Christ consciousness becomes the mode of being. It is impossible to turn back to the old operating system once it has *"crashed."*

Jesus personified or modeled the amalgamation of God and man, or a human being where God dwells inside of man. Remember he said in *John 14:7 "If you have seen me you have seen the Father"* as Jesus did not see himself as separate from God. Christians see God as external from them and worship Him externally by obeying the commandments, attending church, and by paying tithes, etc. Generally speaking, human consciousness up to this point generally sees itself as separate from God, and that God as an entity exists outside of them.

> *After this I looked, and there before me was a door standing open in heaven. And the voice I had first heard speaking to me like a trumpet said, "Come up here, and I will show you what must take place after this." At once I was in the Spirit,*

99

and there before me was a throne in heaven with someone sitting on it. And the one who sat there had the appearance of jasper and carnelian. A rainbow, resembling an emerald, encircled the throne. Surrounding the throne were twenty-four other thrones, and seated on them were twenty-four elders. They were dressed in white and had crowns of gold on their heads. From the throne came flashes of lightning, rumblings and peals of thunder. Before the throne, seven lamps were blazing. These are the seven Spirits of God. Also before the throne there was what looked like a sea of glass, clear as crystal. (Revelation 4:1-6)

The door standing open in heaven is the intuitive mind where Christ consciousness resides. This is an allegorical description for an elevated position in consciousness, heaven representing the metaphorical "upper room" where the disciples met with the Christ. Subtle shifts in our understanding of historical texts may reveal several hidden mysteries including the understanding that the twenty-four elders are the twelve-paired cranial nerves. This is something to think about for sure. There are many excellent resources regarding the Book of Revelation being a mystical narrative of the internal and physical workings of the human brain and body and resulting consciousness. One of them is *Edgar Cayce's On The Revelation* by John Van Auken. (You will learn about the seven churches representing the seven chakras of our energy body). It is an excellent resource.

We may look at Mary, the mother of Jesus, as a historical figure, a virgin who conceived a baby by being *"overshadowed"* by an angel. Mary gave birth to a holy thing, a boy, born in a lowly manger amongst the animals in a barn. This same baby grew to become known as the savior of mankind, and performed all sorts of miracles as he walked the Earth.

Let's forego our historical understanding of Mary for a moment and see Mary as an archetype of the divinely impregnated human being. Mary can be seen as a template, or an overlay for us to see who and what we really are. Archetypical Mary is the feminine nature of the creature within all of humanity. It is the womb of creation that is capable of receiving the seed of the Divine. Mary the womb, the feminine aspect of the entire human field is deemed "virgin" because never before had Divinity found a portal through which to penetrate and deposit the spark/seed of itself. Mary is the portal through which the Divine finds expression in a physical world. We are the corporeal Mary.

Earth is a very special place where the Divine and immaterial (Spirit) has the opportunity to mingle with the physical world. So great was the desire to cohabitate with the material world that a grand plan was forged to ensure and fulfill this desire. Carl Sagan says, *"If you want to bake an apple pie from scratch you must first create the universe."*

Divinity desired cohabitation within the material worlds so the material universe was created. I often say if Divinity walked into the room and wanted to hug someone, kiss a baby, or stroke a dog, it could not unless it had a helpmate. Divinity has no form in the material or physical world unless it enters a body; this helpmate that gives Divinity a means of expression is you, the human being, the human body, the corporeal Mary. Taken literally, this story of the *Immaculate Conception* happens to one woman. Taken metaphorically the story expands. I see that Mary is the human race that has been *"overshadowed"* by something quite divine. As a quantified human, we are so much more than flesh and bone. We have this Divine Spark dwelling within us. Divinity desired expression in matter, therefore an environment that is material and suitable must be created; this is our lovely physical universe.

Jacob, an Old Testament figure, falls asleep on a rock. Rock is a metaphor for intuitively revealed knowledge. Allow me to explain this most important metaphor, as it is a platform to understand the aspect of Divinity indwelling the human body:

In Matthew 16:13-18 Jesus has asked his Disciples this question:

When Jesus came into the coasts of Caesarea Philippi, he asked his disciples, saying, "Whom do men say that I the Son of man am?" And they said, "Some say that thou art John the Baptist: some, Elias; and others, Jeremias, or one of the prophets". He saith unto them, "But whom say ye that I am?" And Simon Peter answered and said, "Thou art the

Christ, the Son of the living God". And Jesus answered and said unto him, "Blessed art thou, Simon Barjona: for flesh and blood hath not revealed it unto thee, but my Father which is in heaven. And I say also unto thee, that thou art Peter, and upon this rock I will build my church; and the gates of hell shall not prevail against it."

Jesus asks his disciples, *"Whom do they say that I am?"* Simon Barjona replies, *"Thou art the Christ"* Jesus replies, *"Flesh and blood hath not revealed this but my Father which is in heaven"* (higher consciousness). Jesus states that no human of flesh and blood revealed this to Peter, the Father in heaven, a state of higher consciousness within man revealed the identity of Christ to Peter. Then Jesus does something interesting, he changes Simon's name (Simon means to listen or listening, hearing) to Peter, which means rock or pebble and metaphorically, rock or pebble represents revealed knowledge from heaven. He goes on to say that he would build his church on this rock; the rock of revealed knowledge—intuited knowledge—not something man has learned intellectually. The word "church" is not in any way referring to a building with a steeple and a congregation or a pastor or priest. The word church in Greek is ecclesia, which means: origin, source, call, called out. It says that WE would be built by the origin, the source and that the gates of hades (limited intellect, lower egocentric or elemental thinking) would not prevail against it. Revealed knowledge calls to us from the origin, the source of all, within.

Now back to Jacob who falls asleep with a "rock" for a pillow, dreams of a ladder where he sees messengers ascending and descending upon it:

When he reached a certain place, he stopped for the night because the sun had set. Taking one of the stones there, he put it under his head and lay down to sleep. He had a dream in which he saw a stairway resting on the earth, with its top reaching to heaven, and the angels of God were ascending and descending on it. There above it stood the LORD, and he said: "I am the LORD, the God of your father Abraham and the God of Isaac. I will give you and your descendants the land on which you are lying. Your descendants will be like the dust of the earth, and you will spread out to the west and to the east, to the north and to the south. All peoples on earth will be blessed through you and your offspring. I am with you and will watch over you wherever you go, and I will bring you back to this land. I will not leave you until I have done what I have promised you.

When Jacob awoke from his sleep, he thought, "Surely the LORD is in this place, and I was not aware of it." He was afraid and said, "How awesome is this place! This is none other than the house of God; this is the gate of heaven." (Genesis 28:11-17)

Jacob goes on to name the place where he laid his head, Bethel or *house of God*. So we see that God's dwelling is not a building but metaphorically is within a state of consciousness. Years ago, while studying this scripture in Hebrew, I saw that the word ladder had "spiral" within the etymology. I had to wonder if this spiral ladder was mysteriously referring to the DNA molecule; Jacob said, *"Surely the Lord is in THIS place* (within our DNA) *and I did not know it."* In other words, the limited intellect did not *know* God. Jacob was speaking as an egocentric man—Jacob means *supplanter* or *one who seizes the place of another* much like the ego has done to our authentic and underlying identity, our origin, Divinity or Spirit. The ego temporarily seizes the place of Divinity while Divinity grows within humanity like the seed planted within the field along with the tares. Jacob did not KNOW that God dwelled within. Later as Jacob struggles with an angelic messenger, we are told his name is also changed from Jacob to Israel, which means: *May God prevail; He struggles with God.* And as egocentric human beings, do we not struggle against the Divine within?

The limited intellect did not know God.

In the grand plan of Divinity wanting to find a helpmate, a suitable biological container or body must be created or *evolved* if you will. Then, a holy impregnation occurs in the manger of our base humanity, and this Spark of the Divine is deposited into our collective consciousness and a synergy; a cooperative effort is covertly established. Do we see this happening through the story of Mary? Other metaphorical emphasis may be placed on the three wise men, the gifts of gold (higher consciousness), frankincense (the priest) and myrrh (suffering), the North Star (divine guidance) etc. Metaphoric inferences are everywhere within the scriptural text.

This spark-like ember of this extra-dimensional energy of Divinity must grow slowly within us lest the delicate circuitry of the human become overwhelmed. The human is unaware that it has been inoculated with something holy, mysterious, and Divine that will expand within our consciousness over millennia. Jacob (the egocentric human) saw this indwelling presence of the Divine within our DNA. Surely God is HERE and we did not know it. Peter could hear the voice of the Divine within him, as it KNEW the Christ. Peter's declaration ushered in the era of the awakened human; the human that is able to hear the voice of God within. It is from this position, the ability to hear the voice of the Divine (the Father in heaven) within, that the church will be built—not a building with a steeple, but a people. We are being built into the habitation of the Most High God (Ephesians 2:22).

And I heard a great voice out of heaven saying, "Behold, the tabernacle of God is with men, and he will dwell with them, and they shall be his people, and God himself shall be with them, and be their God." (Revelation 21:3)

These last few paragraphs may be the most important in the book. It is from this foundational understanding that we see the purpose for our existence.

We are just now becoming aware of this indwelling potential that will morph into *the Christ* as the human counterpart embraces and believes its destiny with the universe. Like the butterfly that emerges from the cocooned caterpillar, transformation occurs from the inside out as we are born again, from a higher position in consciousness or born from above. Again, Emanuel means, "God with man." Jesus within Mary establishes this pattern in the natural to reveal unseen internal spiritual principles. Christ is born in the manger of our humanity and is wrapped in the swaddling clothing of our beautiful biology.

When does this impregnation occur? There may have been many penetrations over the millennia but the most recent significant penetration occurred during the Age of Pisces (the fish). The Age of Pisces began roughly 2000 years ago around the birth of Christ and lasted until recently, within the last 40 years or so. The fish or Vessica Pisces is a symbol of the birth portal and it is during this age that the Divine Spark or Spirit successfully penetrated the material world. The birth of Christ heralds this coming or penetration of the Divine into the material realm within corporeal Mary.

In the Old Testament, it is said that the Spirit came upon them but in the New Testament, we are told the Spirit is within. In the Old Testament, they carried the presence of God on their shoulders in the Ark of the Covenant. In the New Testament, Jesus tells us that

> *God does not dwell in buildings made with hands, and that we are the temple of the Spirit. (1 Corinthians 3:16-17, Acts 7:48, 17:24)*

Furthermore, in Matthew 17:27 the disciples inquired how they should pay the temple tax and Jesus told them to go fishing and that the fish they catch will have a silver coin within its mouth to pay the tax. Metaphorically this is a treasure chest of symbolism. Silver is a symbol of redemption and it is found within the fish, metaphorically the Age of Pisces. The birth of Jesus ushered in the Age of Pisces and redemption would be found within this age. Let's take a look at the definition of redemption, specifically the word redeem and redeemed:

Redeemed: Recovery of something pawned or mortgaged.

Redeem: To recover ownership of by paying a specified sum. The word "redeem" hints at a "buying back" of something that had been mortgaged.

Mortgage: A debt instrument that is secured by the collateral of specified real estate property and that the borrower is obliged to pay back with a predetermined set of payments.

Was Jesus mysteriously stating that the debt owed for the material temple (the body) has been paid during the Age of Pisces? Could this debt owed come in the form of infusing the body material with the body immaterial? Did humanity receive payment in the form of indwelling Divinity? Is this the ultimate redeeming of the body? The pattern of the life of Jesus certainly alludes to this as he raised his dead body from the Earth and became immortal. That is a pattern for us.

> *But if the Spirit of him that raised up Jesus from the dead dwell in you, he that raised up Christ from the dead shall also quicken your mortal bodies by his Spirit that dwells in you. (Romans 8:11)*

The only prerequisite for this quickening is belief. It is the task of the Divine to ransom/redeem a willing mortal body so that in union they may become one flesh. This is what salvation really means. This is what it means to be saved, not to go to some heaven *"up there"* if we do the right things and say the right prayers and belong to the right church. It is to bring the body mortal to a state where it is no longer subject to death.

In the Old Testament story of Joseph we see the account where his jealous older brothers (eleven of them) sold him into slavery in Egypt and told his father that wild animals tore him apart. While in Egypt, Joseph attains a very powerful position within Pharaoh's government. When his brothers sojourn into Egypt they are unaware that their brother Joseph is now entertaining them. Joseph is aware of the impending doom of his family and indeed all of Israel as he is supernaturally foretold of an extensive drought. Before sending his brothers on their way back home, he secretly places a silver cup in a sack of grain and later has the brothers arrested and accused of stealing the silver. The rest of the story is a beautiful reunion between his brothers and ultimately his entire family and nation as they travel to Egypt to be spared of 400 years of terrible drought. Metaphorically this speaks volumes but in short, the nation of Israel is provided for, while under the dominion of the Egyptian regime (egocentricity), with a promise of redemption, the silver chalice hidden within the grain (the Holy Grail—Christ in us). We too will emerge from the drought of the egocentric domination into the Promised Land of redemption.

During the Age of Pisces the potential for the mortal to be redeemed or purchased has occurred. The silver within the mouth of the fish is highly symbolic, the Divine Spark being swallowed up of the Earth realm while its vehicle, the mortal body mastered by ego, learns obedience through the things it suffers all within the belly of humanity. Ironically this belly is called "Sheol" (popularly mistranslated as *hell*.) I often say that there is a hell and this is it. Our mortality offers plenty of hellish experiences from which to learn. Young, old, innocent and guilty, the Earth is a school and it does not discriminate.

I hope you are inoculated with the love for metaphor by perceiving external and historical events as your own internal and unfolding journey. Along with this understanding is my hope and desire to unfold this treasure map even more.

Metaphorical Key:

Mary: Mary is the feminine nature of the creature within all of humanity. It is the womb of creation that is capable of receiving the seed of the Divine. Mary is the physical vehicle through which Divinity finds expression in the material world. Mary partners with Divinity to bring forth the Christ nature in physical form. Remember Christ is an amalgamation of both Divinity and man. Christ is a Hybrid of sorts, a new creation borne in the midst of humanity.

Virgin: Mary is called "virgin" in the physical as she was said to never have been intimate with a man; metaphorically we can infer that this feminine nature within humanity had never been intimate with the Divine and that penetration of our DNA had occurred.

The Book of Revelation: Your evolving and ascending consciousness is revealed.

The Upper Room: Higher consciousness where we meet the Christ.

The Kingdom of Heaven: In order to have a kingdom there is a need for a King. The Kingdom of Heaven is where there is a new ruler within the creature and that new ruler is Divinity. The environment of the kingdom is produced when there is an exchange in consciousness—from egocentric dominated to Divinity inspired. This occurs when the egocentric human willingly yields to its Divine counterpart like a bride to a groom.

Jacob's Ladder: Human DNA.

Rock: Revealed knowledge—knowledge not learned from an external source but revealed internally from the "Father" or the Divine source within.

The Father: The creative potential or "Source", the seed giver, the progenitor, the All in All, the father, the immortal reality, supreme energy that gives life and that animates the body and soul, it is the consciousness of all things big and small.

Silver: Redemption.

Sack of Grain: Harvested crop of humanity. (More in Chapter Eight)

The Fish or Ichthus: The Vessica Pisces is the symbol of two intersecting circles that form the shape of a fish in the overlapped area. Each circle represents a realm or dimensional level and as they merge the center portion is an amalgamation of both realms. The Age of Pisces is identifiable with this symbol. The Vessica Pisces is symbolic of a birth portal or vagina. The advent of the birth of Jesus marked the beginning of the Age of Pisces and the conception of the Christ within mankind.

Summary Points:

- Divinity is like a seed planted in a garden—the garden is the human being.
- Divinity within uses symbolism and metaphor to interpret reality, bypassing limited human reasoning and employing it only when necessary.
- Jesus personified or modeled this amalgamation of God and man.

- The door standing open in "heaven" is in your higher consciousness or metaphorically the "upper room."
- Mary is an archetype of the divinely endowed human.
- Mary (the human) is the portal through which the Divine finds expression in a physical world.
- The word "church" is not in any way referring to a building with a steeple and a congregation or a pastor or priest.
- God's dwelling is not a building but is within a state of consciousness.
- This spark-like ember of the Divine must grow slowly lest the delicate circuitry of the human become overwhelmed.
- We are just now becoming aware of this indwelling potential that will morph into the Christ as the human counterpart embraces and believes its destiny with the universe.
- The only prerequisite for this quickening (immortality) is belief.
- I often say that there is a hell and this is it!

Chapter Eight

The Metaphorical Baptism of Christ

Along with accepting the invitation to be saved several times, I can recall being baptized at least five times in my life; six times if you count being sprinkled as an infant, which is why I did it the second time, in case sprinkling didn't quite count. The third time a few friends and I along with the aid of a youth pastor, jumped off a pier and into a lake. I did it because everyone else was doing it (*pier* pressure). The fourth and fifth times were during a church service. There was a special speaker who was a prophet saying we needed to get right with God. I thought, well maybe I should—I really don't want to go to hell so I did it, and I did it again just in case I didn't mean it the three times before. The last time was in a Jacuzzi outside of our church with my three boys. After all, they were only sprinkled as infants too I thought fearfully, much too young to really know what it meant. We were group dunked.

I deeply appreciate the ritual and more importantly the symbolism of baptism, but back then it was the fear of hell that kept me going back for more. Deep down inside, I, like most fundamentalists, had a fear-based belief in the ritual and a very limited and literal understanding of what it means to be baptized. But once I started to see this and other rituals as metaphors my whole viewpoint changed. John the Baptist introduced water baptism giving to us a tactile act that symbolizes *Divinity's immersion or descent into the material world*, that is, *into human consciousness*. Baptism is not about getting wet, whether it be by sprinkling or dunking, but the ritual does offer a template that shows us Divinity's journey into human consciousness. If we can disengage from the literal act of baptism and the attached dogma, we may see something far more mysterious than perfunctory. We discover that this ritual, when understood metaphorically, is at the heart of our authentic identity as Divinity lowered and immersed into human-hood, then

111

resurrecting from that mortal state, and ascending into immortality. It is cited in scripture that we must be baptized in order to be saved.

Whoever believes and is baptized will be saved, but whoever does not believe will be condemned. (Mark 16:16)

We see there is an edict to be baptized and also to believe. Believe in what? Should we believe in someone else's idea of God killing his Son so that his wrath might be avenged? Should we believe that we have to get sprinkled or dunked to get into heaven? Must we recite a prayer acknowledging that we are sinners?

"Will be condemned" are strong words from which to build a very threatening doctrine. Who wants to be condemned (to hell) and suffer everlasting torment in flames? Can the simple act of being immersed in water really save us?

"We are not human beings having a spiritual experience; we are spiritual beings having a human experience."

The act and ritual of baptism is not so much for egocentric man but rather it is for the Divine nature within man to awaken and to become consciously aware of its own journey. After all it has been immersed into human form, beneath the waters of human consciousness. Likewise, its human partner, the mind, must come to terms with its immortal reality and BELIEVE who and what it is. Otherwise, we have to go around the karmic mountain again sentenced to mortality (the realm of death and decay) until the time of awakening where we finally believe in whom and what we are. Baptism is a profound template found in scripture.

Pierre Teilhard de Chardin says this: *"We are not human beings having a spiritual experience; we are spiritual beings having a human experience."* And this we are. At the core of our very existence lies Spirit, our Divinity. Like the story of Joseph, our Father has placed on our spiritual framework a coat of many colors that reflects our fascinating biology. Divinity has been clothed with man.

Ken Carey, in his groundbreaking book, *The Third Millennium* says that the Divine aspect of us has fallen asleep under the spell of matter (or the material realm). He says, *"And so you chose to sleep for a while, allowing the materializing influences to flow freely in and around the developing species. But while your sleep itself was intended, the excessive dominance of materiality during humankind's development was not."*

This "developing species" is the coming together of Divinity and humanity—a new consciousness forming within the womb of the earth, a new creation, a being that is both God and man. Apparently having a "physical" experience endows Divinity with sensory overload. Song of Solomon 8:4 speaks of *awakening the beloved but not before the time.* Who is this sleeper? We are presently in the midst of this great awakening and so we must understand that the sleeper is a twofold being: human consciousness that is unaware that it is cohabiting with Divinity within one body and Divinity that has been lulled to sleep by the human's physical senses in materiality.

Again, this simple act of baptism in water represents this Divine Spark being lowered into human consciousness, holding its Divine breath while they both become fully acquainted and exercised within with the creature-hood of duality. And this *baptism* we are told is necessary if we are to be "saved." Divinity must be immersed in humanity if it is to court, marry and ultimately resurrect its human counterpart.

As we discussed earlier, human biology was once again inoculated with the Divine Spark during the Age of Pisces. We have learned that the human became a bi-dimensional being as the sphere of the material realm overlapped the celestial realm creating the Vessica Pisces or the birth portal (the fish or Ichthus as Christianity calls it). These overlapping spheres that form the birth portal indicate that we are bi-dimensional beings capable of terrestrial and celestial habitation. Consciousness now inhabits the place of overlapping dimensions and is both God and man as celestial seed is deposited into the birth portal. The advent of the coming of the Christ is an occurrence of celestial energy penetrating the terrestrial. This advent is the birth of Divinity within humanity, the babe in the manger.

As this celestial Spark-seed holds its breath (or its immortal memory) it is a silent partner in humanity in order to be fully invested in creature-hood. We simply have a gap (the dead zone) between our immortal reality and our humanity that prohibits us from accessing our memories from another dimensional vibratory range. It's like dreaming, and from within the dream we have limited access to reality. But as we awaken, we exit the mist of slumber into alert habitation of our world. And so it will be as we experience spiritual awakening. We will remember.

So from the Age of Pisces until we enter into the Age of Aquarius, this amalgamation of celestial and terrestrial energies has been incubating within the world of matter. The celestial energy came to the material realm within the human body as a small spark initially. But slowly over the centuries, has been increasing as evidenced by the change and growth in our consciousness. Consciousness precedes all manifestation, or in other words, you have to believe it before you see it. Change must incubate within our consciousness before we see outward manifestation. This is at the heart of the parable of the Mustard seed that I mentioned in Chapter Five.

> *Again he said, "What shall we say the kingdom of God is like, or what parable shall we use to describe it? It is like a mustard seed, which is the smallest seed you plant in the ground. Yet when planted, it grows and becomes the largest of all garden plants, with such big branches that the birds of the air can perch in its shade." (Mark 4:30-32)*

Another parable of something beginning very small is the parable of the yeast within the dough:

> *He told them still another parable: "The Kingdom of heaven is like yeast that a woman took and mixed into a large amount of flour until it worked all through the dough." (Matthew 13:33)*

Yeast has a quality that causes dough to "rise" as in resurrection. Conversely, there was a time when all the yeast was to be cleaned from the house (metaphorically your body) during the feast of unleavened bread. This was metaphor for us purposefully losing the ability to "rise" or to ascend beyond the bounds of the gap, where we consciously occupy the material world without memory of our true identity, our immortal origin.

This Divine Spark would one day be "redeemed." To be fully invested into creature-hood is an absolutely necessary component as we develop into the pattern of Christ. It is said that Jesus was *"tempted in every way" (Hebrews 4:15)* but found the higher path not to sin—that is, not to live as an egocentric human.

It is necessary to understand the word sin. Sin is simply this; it is the environment created while living according to and under the thumb of ego. It is not whether you cheat, lie, steal, kill etc. These acts are by-products of the realm where ego is in charge of man. It is where the serpent is entangled within the tree of our human consciousness and is not free to ascend. Sin is the whole environment where acts like these occur. Jesus did not live according to the ego but rather did only what he heard his Father say (revealed knowledge from within). Jesus did not follow his own ego but was led by the eternal presence within. This is the way we are to follow—a way that produces another dimension where duality is not the driving factor.

> *And that I do nothing on my own but speak just what the Father has taught me. The one who sent me is with me; he has not left me alone, for I always do what pleases him. (John 8:28-29)*

This celestial Spark is like a seed falling from a mature tree that must die or at the very least become dormant until it is planted in darkness where it germinates and descends further downward. Here it accesses the treasures of darkness *(Isaiah 45:3)* found within the rich soil of our humanity and creates a root system. Then suddenly it turns skyward, ascends and breaks the plane of the Earth. In Christianity we were taught about the treasures of darkness (we were told they were literal riches from the ungodly or the *unsaved*) being turned over to the "righteous ones." Inverting reality teaches us a different story. We are being given the treasures of a mortal albeit futile and darkened existence, reaping the benefits of being fully human. While Divinity is dormant, the human becomes fully adept in duality, knowing good from evil. To experience and create the colorful tapestry of duality is absolutely necessary for our education as God-men.

I will give you the treasures of darkness, riches stored in secret places. (Isaiah 45:3)

(The "secret places" is the vault within that stores valuable emotional currency. More on that later.)

So it is with this Spark of Divinity invested into humanity, until the human repents (repenting means to change the way that you think, from egocentric to Divinity-centric) and believes in its own power in conjunction with the Spark to resurrect or to "save" the body. This body is a necessary vehicle (helpmate) for Divinity as it begins to navigate the material universe. Earth is just an incubator of Christ consciousness, a giant terrarium of sorts. The Earth is growing a crop that is seeded and harvested again and again and again. Signs from former crops (civilizations) remain as stonework (pyramids, Stonehenge etc.) that gives testimony to advanced consciousness that formerly walked the planet.

The ritual of baptism is for the benefit of this Spark of Divinity that grows over the millennia, practicing the act until one day it remembers who and what it is, awakening within the sleeper under the spell of human-hood, and entering into the harvest period.

Once we grasp the metaphorical value of baptism, we will understand our own creative potential as this Spark of Divinity immersed into humanity. No longer will we be sentenced to the karmic cycle repeating lifetimes holding our Divine breath under the waters of human consciousness. We must emerge and believe in the Christ within and in this incredible potential that is presently couched in human-hood if we are to enter into true salvation. Jesus walked above human consciousness when he walked on water. He bids us, *"Come."*

Hebrews 6:1-3 says this:

Therefore leaving the principles of the doctrine of Christ, let us go on unto perfection; not laying again the foundation of repentance from dead works, and of faith toward God, of the doctrine of baptisms, and of laying on of hands, and of resurrection of the dead, and of eternal judgment. And this will we do, if God permit.

This scripture announces the end of doctrines and a new dispensation of awareness in perfection telling us to leave behind several key foundational issues. One of them is the doctrine of Baptisms (another is Faith toward God and Eternal judgment—that's another teaching!). We practiced the template of baptism repeatedly over the centuries and now we see we are to set those perfunctory, elementary and foundational doctrines aside that we may move on to perfection. This particular doctrine was indeed foundational to our understanding, albeit one-dimensional. Viewing baptism as metaphorical will greatly enhance our understanding of the journey of Divinity into our human consciousness. It is another prime example of leaving the history to embrace the mystery.

When all the people were being baptized, Jesus was baptized too. And as he was praying, heaven was opened and the Holy Spirit descended on him in bodily form like a dove. And a voice came from heaven: "You are my Son, whom I love; with you I am well pleased." (Luke 3:21-22)

I baptize you with water for repentance. But after me comes one who is more powerful than I, whose sandals I am not worthy to carry. He will baptize you with the Holy Spirit and fire. (Matthew 3:11)

Even Jesus in his thirty years prior to baptism was immersed into human consciousness. Baptizing with *"water for repentance"* heralds the change in human consciousness as we change the way we think. Coming up and out of the water symbolizes an end to the age of duality, the age where we have learned to discern good from evil as we have thought and acted according to our limited and dense human consciousness.

It is said then that Jesus will baptize us with the Holy Spirit and fire. So many in Christianity say that this is speaking in tongues but it is far more mysterious than that. The baptism in Spirit will herald a change in our molecular makeup, as Divinity has infiltrated not only our consciousness but our biology as well. No more will we have our future dominated by limitation as we see our bodies ail from the sickness and disease that is typical for this dispensation. Rather, the coming up and out of the waters of spiritual baptism represents a transition from mortal to immortal.

> *So will it be with the resurrection of the dead. The body that is sown is perishable, it is raised imperishable; it is sown in dishonor, it is raised in glory; it is sown in weakness, it is raised in power; it is sown a natural body, it is raised a spiritual body. If there is a natural body, there is also a spiritual body.*
>
> *So it is written: "The first man Adam became a living being"; the last Adam, a life-giving Spirit. The spiritual did not come first, but the natural, and after that the spiritual. The first man was of the dust of the earth; the second man is of heaven. As was the earthly man, so are those who are of the earth; and as is the heavenly man, so also are those who are of heaven. And just as we have borne the image of the earthly man, so shall we bear the image of the heavenly man.*
>
> *I declare to you, brothers and sisters, that flesh and blood cannot inherit the kingdom of God, nor does the perishable inherit the imperishable. Listen, I tell you a mystery: We will not all sleep, but we will all be changed—in a flash, in the twinkling of an eye, at the last trumpet. For the trumpet will sound, the dead will be raised imperishable, and we will be changed. For the perishable must clothe itself with the imperishable, and the mortal with immortality. When the perishable has been clothed with the imperishable, and the mortal with immortality, then the saying that is written will come true: "Death has been swallowed up in victory."* (1 Corinthians 15:42-54)

Humanity is rapidly approaching this change in consciousness. The earth has served its purpose by providing for us a backdrop in which to learn and mature. It has not been a mistake or in vain. It has been a purposeful cocoon in which the Divine has purposed to bring forth a new creation that is both God and man.

As for the threat of hell for not being baptized—metaphorically speaking, in order for the Divine to acquire a material body, it must first court a helpmate—the human being. It and the human together must be fully *exercised* in the knowledge of good and evil in order to go on to immortality. There is divine purpose in dualism as it teaches us how to manage our emotions. Emotions accrue a powerful energetic currency that we must learn to spend wisely. If we never come to an awakened state then we suffer the dream to continue. This is the karmic cycle of life and death, life and death, life and death. That is hell—never entering into the imperishable life that is promised.

In summary, it is important to see the act of baptism as metaphoric rather than a literal act. When baptism is performed it serves the purpose of awakening the Divinity within humanity of its choice to be willfully immersed into mortality within human consciousness. This act of willful immersion into humanity comes with a price that must be paid by the Divine. It is necessary to acquire a body. There will not be salvation (resurrecting to immortality) unless there is immersion into the waters of humanity. It must forget its identity while mortal until the time of awakening and not one minute before:

> *I charge you, O ye daughters of Jerusalem, by the roes, and by the hinds of the field, that ye stir not up, nor awake my love, till he please. (Song of Solomon 2:7)*

Summary Points:

* Metaphorically, water represents human consciousness.
* John the Baptist introduced baptism giving to us a tactile act that symbolizes Divinity's immersion or descent into the material world that is synonymous with human consciousness.
* Baptism metaphorically represents Divinity's journey (immersion) into human consciousness.
* This simple act of baptism in water represents this Divine Spark being lowered into human consciousness, holding its Divine breath while the egocentric human aspect becomes fully

acquainted and exercised within with the creature-hood of duality.

- This celestial Spark-seed must hold its Divine breath (its immortal memory) as a silent partner in humanity in order to be fully invested in creature-hood.

- So it is with this Spark of Divinity invested into humanity, until the human repents (repenting means to change the way that you think, from ego to eternal) and believes in its own power in conjunction with the Spark to resurrect or to "save" the body.

- This body is a necessary vehicle (helpmate) for Divinity as it begins to navigate the material universe.

- Earth is just an incubator of Christ consciousness.

- The ritual of baptism is to help awaken slumbering Divinity within man.

- This "developing species" is the confluence of Divinity and humanity—a new consciousness forming within the womb of the earth, a new creation, a being that is both God and man.

- To repent means to change the way that you think.

- The earth has served its purpose by providing for us a back drop in which to learn and mature. It has not been a mistake or in vain. It has been a purposeful cocoon in which the Divine has purposed to bring forth a new creation that is both God and man.

Chapter Nine

Metaphorical Communion

I'll never forget the first time I was denied communion. Generally speaking, in Wisconsin, where I was born and raised, you were either Catholic or Lutheran. Down the street from us was a rather large family with ten children and two parents living in a three-bedroom home—they were Catholic. They had a huge picnic table in their kitchen that they would pile around for mealtime. One Sunday I went to church with my friend, Mary, and her nine siblings. It was the first time I had ever been to a Catholic Mass. I remember going to the altar with Mary where she received the wafer and sipped from the goblet. I was kneeling with my mouth open just like Mary but he passed me by withholding the wafer and giving it to the next person. The priest with the cup also passed me by. I stood up and turned around just a little confused but returned to the pew along with everyone else. For the first time in my young life I began to see that Catholics and Protestants were different and I felt a little shunned. I learned though, not to approach an altar in a Catholic church for communion again. In my young mind I thought they just did not like us Lutherans.

I really didn't understand communion anyway. I knew it wasn't really a body that they were eating, just a funny cracker. As I grew older I still questioned the ritual—why did Jesus tell us to eat his body and drink his blood? It wasn't until my mid-forties that I began to see communion as something mystical, again, and not something perfunctory or even something we needed to "take" literally.

I thought, *how many millions of people take communion and have little or no understanding of it?* When I began to see communion metaphorically I had another dramatic shift in my understanding. Communion is a template that overlays our journey as the Spark of Divinity investing itself into humanity. This ritual, when practiced, serves to gently remind and to awaken the sleeper of Divinity within us.

Let's take a look at communion also known as the *"Last Supper."* I prefer to call it, *"come-union."* At the Last Supper, Jesus was with his disciples sharing a meal together. He told them this:

> *And he took bread, gave thanks and broke it, and gave it to them, saying, "This is my body given for you; do this in remembrance of me." (Luke 22:19)*

Do this in remembrance of me - the Christ within.

> *While they were eating, Jesus took bread, and when he had given thanks, he broke it and gave it to his disciples, saying, "Take and eat; this is my body." (Matthew 26:26)*

Let's explore the symbolic meaning of not only bread but also broken bread:

Jesus said, *"I am the bread that came down from heaven" (John 6:51).* In Matthew 13 Jesus teaches about the parable of the Wheat and the Tares. We see that there is a crop that has been growing, comes to maturity, is separated from the weeds, harvested, brought into the barn and threshed. The teaching ends by stating that the grain is in the barn and that this harvest is the *"end of the age."*

This is a beautiful and parabolic template. We see that during this present age, there is a crop growing that will be harvested or separated from the soil of the Earth, threshed and the grain is set in the barn. That's it—the parable ends there. But grain gathered into the barn is not good for anything if it just sits in the barn. I thought to myself, if one age ends after the grain has been harvested and stored, then what happens in the next age? What do we do with wheat grain? Make it into bread?

In this cryptic message Jesus was stating that he came from another dimension, another consciousness, from an "age" beyond where we presently are. *"I am the bread that came down from heaven."* Jesus had already been through the process of the earth school and is a returning alumnus of sorts to help a graduating class. Beings that have achieved this level of consciousness are called

"Christ." And again, there have been many Christed beings and masters that have walked the face of the earth even before the birth of Jesus.

This giant terrarium has been incubating the Christ seed within humanity for thousands of years. This seed is growing and bearing fruit that comes from maturity—fit for the next dimensional level. Each dimension carries its own specific frequency and the Earth's frequency is comprised mainly of fear, a very low vibratory range. The message from Jesus of love and non-judgment will help propel us out from fear and fear-based mentalities that typify elementary human thought and prime us for entrance into the age to come (another dimensional level). Humanity is beginning to change the way it thinks and perceive reality. Not only will we experience this *"harvest"* but remember in the natural world, harvesting a field may occur many, many times. Like a school, we are not the only graduating class. The Earth, like a garden has been seeded and harvested *many times.*

In the Last Supper, Jesus referred to the bread that he was holding as his "body" and then he *"broke it."* Metaphorically, Jesus was telling us that his immortal status was surrendered or broken, when he descended dimensional levels, and wrapped his Divine self in this body of death or mortality. His immortal body was *"broken"* for us. Viewing this as a template we see that it was our immortal or celestial body that was likewise broken or at least surrendered while Divinity within us sojourns into humanity. *We must re-member.*

As a human race endowed with Divinity we must, for a time, forget whom we are in order to be fully invested into creature-hood. Our human senses get us drunk and our egocentric self becomes addicted and lost in sensory overload in a world fueled by good and evil—or duality. Like a seed in the ground that never germinates, we need activation to sprout. We need a savior to come remind us of who and what we are and to set a pattern or "way" for our own awakening and ascension. We may see this historically which is not wrong, but Jesus modeled something within ourselves that we cannot see. The Christ's appearing is within our upper room—descending down from heaven, a body of immortality broken, but eventually redeemed as this egoist life of self, surrenders.

In the ritual of *come-union,* the broken bread is placed in the mouth and swallowed, it descends down the throat, a metaphor in scripture for the grave or death *(Romans 3:13)* and ultimately ends up *in the belly.* The belly represents the material mortal realm of death, and is synonymous with what Christians call Hell. The broken bread (Christ nature) is swallowed into mortality—the immortal body "broken" for us. Jesus called this place *"Gehenna"* the place where rubbish is burned. It is a metaphoric example of lower living, or living in a place subjected to the continual barrage of fear. *Fundamentalism is rubbish.*

Within the story of Jonah is another comparable template. Jonah was swallowed up in the belly of the great fish. Jesus even compared himself to Jonah:

> *For as Jonah was three days and three nights in the belly of a huge fish, so the Son of Man will be three days and three nights in the heart of the earth. (Matthew 12:40)*

Metaphorically, the story of the great fish is the Age of Pisces that swallowed the Christ, brought him into death (the mortal realm) until the time when death gives way to life. This age is when and where humanity was penetrated by the Divine Spark and subjected itself to mortality and duality until the end of the age. We have now entered into the Age of Aquarius. Jesus alluded to this transition of the ages and tells us that the coming Age of Aquarius is when we would experience the shift out of egocentric based mentalities and begin to build the vibrational bridge from one age to the next. We know that thought precipitates all change and in this transitional time between the ages, human thought is changing.

In Chapter Five we briefly touched on the story of the Passover lamb. Metaphorically, the Christ is the Passover lamb, the lamb slain before the foundation of the world (as it is written in *Revelation 13:8).* Jesus modeled for us the lamb that was slain and this death of the lamb is Divinity within ALL subjecting its immortal self to the realm of death, mortality. Becoming human, Divinity willingly lays down its immortal self and wraps itself in the grave clothes of humanity. Even before the world was, this plan was forged and agreements were made.

Jesus said his body was broken—the broken bread of *come-union*. Let's go further and connect some more dots:

In *Mark 14:12-16* we are told of a great mystery.

And the first day of unleavened bread, when they killed the Passover, his disciples said unto him, where wilt thou that we go and prepare that thou may eat the Passover? And he sent forth two of his disciples, and he said unto them, Go ye into the city, and there shall meet you a man bearing a pitcher of water: follow him. And where ever he shall go in, say ye to the good man of the house, The Master said, Where is the guest chamber, where I shall eat the Passover with my disciples? And he will show you a large upper room furnished and prepared: there make ready for us. And his disciples went forth, and came into the city, and found as he had said unto them: and they made ready the Passover.

The disciples were asking where they, as good Jews, would celebrate and eat the Passover meal with Jesus. Jesus told them to

"Go ye into the city, and there shall meet you a man bearing a pitcher of water: follow him."

This is a cryptic message about the Age of Aquarius that would come upon humanity in roughly two thousand years. In the constellation that reflects the Aquarian age we see a person bearing a pitcher of water and some depictions show the water being poured out from the pitcher.

Water represents human consciousness and it is being poured out of us. We are the containers of water (human consciousness) so this hints at us being emptied of human consciousness. Also, in the account of the Wedding at Cana the water in the six stone pitchers is turned into wine. We are changing from the inside out.

Aquarius

Remember the blood from the Passover lamb was placed on the doorposts (portals) so that the firstborn sons did not have to die. If we want to celebrate the firstborn (that is humanity in our physical, mortal form) not having to die, then we must look to the Age of Aquarius and go to the upper room (higher consciousness). The Passover lamb symbolizes man's Divine nature that willingly entered into death, surrendering immortality by becoming mortal, and demonstrating pure non-resistance for the journey.

The lamb's blood was to be placed on the doorposts so that the firstborn male children of the Israelites in captivity to Pharaoh did not have to experience death. God initiated this curse to move Pharaoh into submission and as Moses said, to *"let my people go!"* They had been indentured for four hundred years and they desired to return to their homeland. Then in the New Testament, they wanted to practice, as good Jews, the ritual of the Passover lamb (again symbolizing the firstborn sons not having to die). Jesus told them to look for the man bearing the pitcher of water (metaphor for the Age of Aquarius) and go to the upper room. It is from this elevated place in consciousness, the upper room, that we will begin our migration free from the laws that govern this dimensional level, and will ultimately free us from a lower position in human consciousness.

We are presently poised to enter into the "upper room" (higher consciousness) having "followed" the person bearing the pitcher of water, or the Age of Aquarius.

126

We are presently poised to enter into the "upper room" (higher consciousness) having "*followed*" the person bearing the pitcher of water, or the Age of Aquarius. *Followed* means that we have understood the inference of Jesus pointing to the Age of Aquarius and thereby understood the mystery of his words. The ritual of *come-union* shows us that the broken bread (the immortal Christ nature in submission to death by becoming mortal) is swallowed up into *the belly* that is, the mortal Earth realm becoming human. This ritual nudges us into awakening—to see that it is *we who have surrendered our immortal status having entered into human-hood and that it is time to awaken and remember the reason for the journey and our underlying identity as Divinity.*

In summary, the bread descends down the portal of death into the belly of mortality—this Divine being was willing to set aside its immortality, picking up a mortal body for the purposes of establishing a pattern for us, to remind us, to awaken the latent Divinity within of our own journey. Scripture says of Jesus that he is the *"firstborn of many brethren."* We are the Divine Spark that agreed before the foundation of the world to forfeit our eternal nature and to invest ourselves into mortality. We do this so that we may synergize with a material helpmate that is flesh and blood body. Through the pattern of the Last Supper we take the bread and wine into ourselves and we *"do this in remembrance of me."* That "me" that Jesus referred to is the Spark of the Divine, latent in everyone, that has temporarily gone to sleep and is dreaming the dream of mortality. The ritual is practiced until we remember who and what we are. Broken "bread" descends down through the portal of death and rests in the belly, mortality. It is a ritual practiced to remind us of our journey from eternity into mortality to retrieve a body as a helpmate for this immaterial to navigate material realms. Divinity courts the mortal vessel endowed with the Spark and wins for Himself a wife, a partner, a helpmate to co-create, pro-create a being that is both God and Man.

This is a very stout concept and one that will absolutely change reality, as we know it. This is merely a taste of this mystical understanding.

After the death and resurrection of Jesus, he appeared walking on the road to Emmaus. The men he walked with did not recognize him:

> *As they approached the village to which they were going, Jesus continued on as if he were going farther. But they urged him strongly, "Stay with us, for it is nearly evening; the day is almost over." So he went in to stay with them. When he was at the table with them, he took bread, gave thanks, broke it and began to give it to them. Then their eyes were opened and they recognized him, and he disappeared from their sight. (Luke 24:28-31)*

It was not until the bread was *broken* that their eyes were "opened" and they recognized Christ. This powerful ritual will do the same for us as we break bread and remember, Christ in you, has come from heaven to Earth. Joy to the world, the Lord is come. Let Earth receive her King!

Summary Points:

- Communion is something mystical and not something perfunctory or even something we need to "take" literally.
- Like a giant terrarium, the Earth has been incubating the Christ seed within humanity for thousands of years. This seed is growing and bearing fruit that comes from maturity—fit for the next dimensional level.
- Each dimension carries its own specific frequency and the Earth's frequency is comprised mainly of fear, a very low vibratory range.
- The message from Jesus of love and non-judgment will help propel us out from fear and fear-based mentalities that typify elementary human thought and prime us for entrance into the age to come.
- Not only will we experience this "harvest" but it is important to say that this has happened many, many times before us. Like a school, we are not the only graduating class. The Earth, like a garden, has been seeded and harvested many times.
- In the Last Supper, Jesus referred to the bread that he was holding as his "body" and then he "broke it." Metaphorically,

Jesus was telling us that his immortal status was surrendered or broken, when he descended dimensional levels, and wrapped his Divinity in this body of death or mortality.

- We needed someone to come remind us of who and what we are and to show a pattern or "way" of ascension. That pattern or way is fearlessness. The pattern teaches us how to bring the life of the ego willingly into a place of death as master of the body so that it may resurrect a servant to Divinity.

- In the constellation of Aquarius, we see a person bearing a pitcher of water and some depictions show the water being poured out from the pitcher. Again, water represents human consciousness and it is being poured out of us. We are the containers of water (human consciousness).

- Divinity courts the mortal vessel endowed with the Spark and wins for Himself a wife, a partner, a helpmate to co-create, pro-create a being that is both God and Man.

Chapter Ten

Latent Divinity and Divine Intrusions

As we have learned, we are endowed organically with a Spark of Divinity. We know that this measure of Spirit, this Spark, has been with us for eons, nesting, incubating and developing intrinsically. The scripture alludes to this as the treasure in earthen vessels, the treasure found and buried within a field, a mustard seed planted and growing in a garden, a farmer sowing seed in his field, a woman mixing yeast into dough that leavens the whole of it, and the merchant looking for a pearl of great price.

Divinity has invested the invaluable into the temporal: the eternal Spirit into a mortal frame. There have been many investments of Divinity into mortality in our human historical timeline, a little bit at a time so as to not overwhelm the delicate human nervous system. This deposit is carried into many lifetimes. Bit by bit, the initial deposit attracts interest until the principal accrued overtakes the initial investment. In this case, the interest is added down throughout history as *moments of intrusion* of the Divine into the material framework of man. Day by day, and millennia after millennia we can see the consciousness of the human being advance and retreat like breath in lungs, retaining what is valuable and expelling the useless. Progress is made in such ways as human consciousness is always on the move, albeit restrained in part by the standards, culturalisms and doctrines of each passing age.

Many of these occasions have peppered the historical human course with unexplainable phenomena taking place in and around mankind. The Cane Ridge Revival in Kentucky, August 1801 was one such time. It is recorded that thousands upon thousands of people were struck with various and unusual physical manifestations such as shaking, roaring, jerking and falling unconscious, some of these episodes lasting from one to twenty four hours. People were said to have had to hold onto the trunks of trees to maintain some semblance of equilibrium. This event was just one of many more to come. The Shaker and Quaker religions were named for such movements. In the early 1900's the Welsh Revival and Azusa Street Revival were in full swing with thousands of people speaking in tongues among other odd manifestations. One of the most recent of these happenings occurred in the 1990's in Toronto, Canada as well as many other locations around the globe including Pensacola (Brownsville), Florida. The happening in Toronto was called the *"Toronto Blessing"* and included many of the same manifestations as what occurred in Cane Ridge as well as *"holy laughter"* where people could not stop laughing. I would have been a skeptic and cynic had I not experienced these happenings in Toronto and Brownsville as well as numerous occasions in Houston, Dallas, and Austin and in my hometown of College Station, TX. The common and continual prayer of those desiring to experience this movement was the phrase, *"More Lord, more."* Many times I stood for hours it seemed seeking this strange power to come over me. I repeatedly stood in prayer lines for someone to put their hands on me and pray for me to "receive" it.

Emotional baggage, hurt and pain from the past disappeared and what seemed like "downloads" of revelatory information began to happen.

Once a young man had me turn the palms of my hands upward while he gently centered his hands over mine, barely touching. I experienced something like an electrical current coming down from his hands to mine and into my body and I began to jerk with wavelike pulses that came into my abdomen. I still experience it today, more than 15 years later. During these times of Divine intrusion, something otherworldly seemed to be taking place. Emotional baggage, hurt and pain from the past disappeared and what seemed like "downloads" of revelatory information began to happen. I had moments similar to the experience in Chapter One where I lost entire blocks of dogmatic understanding, including losing the meaning of the word "saved". I have heard it explained that during these times a higher dimensional energy leaked through to our dimension through various portals of access and overlap. I am unsure of exactly what it is and how it happens; all I know for sure is that I and countless of other people were dramatically and forever changed by it. Many of them eventually departed institutionalized religion whereas others are still seeking the *"more"* within the religious system.

Prior to Cane Ridge Revival there were occurrences written about in the Bible where ordinary people heard God speak, saw angels, fell on their faces as though they were dead and some had hair that turned white—these moments of Divine intrusion made a definite impact in human physiology.

Have we been experiencing some sort of spiritual inoculation? Have our bodies been tweaked by Divinity encoding or activating unused parts of our DNA during these moments of intrusion? If it wasn't always there, then when did it first come in? There may be a lot of theories out there and I would like to offer mine.

One day while driving down the highway, I was struck with a thought about the missing link. First, I need to say that it is probably obvious that I am not a scientist. I want to offer information that has been intuited and you will most likely never see it published in a scientific magazine. Interestingly, this information came to me suddenly while traveling over a bridge. I was thinking about the missing link, nothing specific, just pondering what it was. As you may know, it is theorized that there is a missing skeletal example in our evolutionary ladder between what is deemed to be animal and man. Neanderthal, considered to be animal, is the last example before this gap between it and man and was considered to be instinctual rather than intellectual. It was functioning out of the first of our three brains, the reptilian brain.

Divinity has invested the invaluable into the temporal; the eternal Spirit into a mortal frame.

When intuited information comes to me, it does not necessarily come in the form of language, sometimes it comes in the form of an impression or vision. I will see images or feel feelings, and sometimes words are the vehicle for such information. As I drove I saw this chain of skeletal examples with a gap toward the end of the chain. I knew intuitively that Divinity had, all along been keeping a thoughtful eye on our developing species, gently tweaking the creation and causing subtle shifts in our evolutionary processes.

When I say the word *tweaking* it is because I saw fingers gently flick the creature each time an adjustment had to be made in our consciousness that ultimately resulted in changes within our physiological makeup. These changes manifest through our skeletal remains. The creature was evolving *and it was on schedule*. Then, with careful regard to the species, a major shift is planned for the creature. Divinity sees that the creature has the abilities necessary and desirable—it can build, think and reason instinctually and for survival but lacks inspiration and imagination, the qualities needed for god-hood. Divinity waited for the portal to open and with careful precision, the DNA molecule was penetrated by this quintessential element, and the creature became endowed with SPIRIT. In this moment, a quantum leap of epic proportion occurs and leaves a gap in skeletal remains. The skeletal example is perceived as *missing* in the evolutionary ladder because the creature had moved from animal to human. *There is no missing link—it was never there.* Somehow the consciousness of the creature experienced a dramatic and immediate upgrade, which produced a new creature. The former vessel, Neanderthal, then passed away or was absorbed into this new breed. Who can say for sure? All we know is that the "link" between animal and man is not there.

Divinity waited for the portal to open and with careful precision the DNA molecule was penetrated by this quintessential element, and the creature became endowed with SPIRIT.

I feel that Divinity initially penetrated the bloodline somewhere along this point in linear time when Neanderthal was the premiere being on the planet, possibly when the portal, the constellation Pisces, was prominent in one of the many previous appearances during the precession of the equinox. The precession of the equinox is a 24,000 year cycle when each of the twelve constellations appears prominently in the eastern sky every 2,000 year (approximately). That penetration produced a being that was inspired, leading to the modern human. This being had imagination and produced art with vision as it was endowed with the Spark of the Divine. All along, Divinity was intently watching and observing the progress of its investment into the material plane, carefully making necessary adjustments in order for the creature to become a suitable habitation for *itself.* Many, many times had this and other creatures been the observer's object of interest, and, by the sheer magnitude of its thoughtful gaze and powerful intent, caused this leap in our physical and conscious evolution.

We are anointed beings practicing Divinity unconsciously in a mortal environment.

This endowment of inspiration, or imagination if you will, is unique to all other forms of life on Earth. We are *anointed beings practicing Divinity* unconsciously in a mortal environment.

So there it is. Who sits around and thinks up stuff like that? I have to say that when information like this comes to me, it really doesn't originate from within the linear mind. It comes from beyond thinking, from a place of knowing. I may not have everything exactly right as information such as this passes through the mind that utilizes the intellect to interpret what it has intuited. However, I feel it is close to the reality of our evolutionary process.

There is something called the "Generations of Isis" which is the word origin of Genesis. There is understanding that there was a woman named Isis who was born into a single-browed race of beings; However, Isis had two brows and was highly intelligent. It is said that from this woman and six others like her that the modern human emerged.

Fundamentalist Christianity has willingly placed itself in a dogmatic "time out" where its consciousness has become an oxbow lake in the still waters of literalism.

With this viewpoint, it becomes easier to bridge the gap between creationism and evolution. Can they co-exist? Fundamentalist Christianity has willingly placed itself in a dogmatic "time out" where its consciousness has become an oxbow lake in the still waters of literalism. Most fundamentalists deny the evolution theory because they believe the earth is only six thousand years old.

Some had such profound visitation from something deemed otherworldly and did not move past the point when the incursion happened, never growing or advancing beyond the exceptional moment.

Consider for a moment some religious Christian sects that experienced these Divine moments of intrusion. Some had such profound visitation from something deemed otherworldly and did not move past the point when the incursion happened, never growing or advancing beyond the exceptional moment. Some Fundamentalist Christian denominations that experienced incredible supernatural manifestations decades ago still maintain the same dogmatic guidelines as back then—women cannot wear makeup, pants or cut their hair. Some other sects refuse to use electricity or motorized vehicles. It is almost as if they feel that by maintaining the atmosphere of the initial visitation, they can expect another one.

If we do not allow for adjustment in our consciousness then we will be as the Neanderthal is considered today—Extinct.

I spoke with a well-known author and evangelist and he said this to me:

"If what you say is true then my life's work has been in vain."

136

Up until that point I could have said my life's ministry and message had been in vain too, but now I consider it a necessary part of my education on planet Earth. We cannot despise the womb that gives us birth, whatever form the structure takes. For some the womb is science. For others it is religion. I had to let go of my ministry and reputation in order to move on from fundamentalism.

I have since experienced countless moments of intrusion. An intrusion in the natural world is liquid rock that forms beneath the surface of the Earth and pushes up through access points that form mountain ranges. We learned in Chapter Seven that rock symbolizes revealed knowledge. These "high places" in the Earth are formed at moments of intrusion from something deep within our Earth (metaphorically, our DNA and or consciousness). Like the microcosm of the Earth, the human receives revelation when a highpoint needs to be established and if there is *present access*. No wonder mountains are so beautiful and magnificent. We see in scripture that many a mountain or high place is visited and an increase in spiritual awareness, understanding and knowledge has been the result.

The mind must be accessible for such an increase. Magma finds access points in the Earth's crust from which to intrude—but fear, through continued egocentricity, closes us off. The need to be right keeps us isolated within our thick crusty places in consciousness, overlaid continually with fear and reinforced with dogma. One must be open to the possibilities. Many reformation movements that Christians embrace today came from extraordinary moments of intrusion by the Divine into human consciousness—Martin Luther, Albert Finney and John Wesley to name a few—all bringing insight and enlightenment to humanity.

Jesus was a revolutionary. He bucked the status quo system of Judaism and he was crucified for it. Viewed metaphorically, he set a pattern for us to break down the barriers of dogmatic and unquestioned belief, ritual and ceremony. Paraphrasing, Jesus said of his persecutors to his disciples, *"If they did this to me they will do it to you."* Those ambassadors that carry this revolutionary message will face the firing squad of religion, just as (Saul) Paul persecuted and killed the followers of Christ, the harbingers of change.

Fundamentalism must be "right." If not, they are threatened repetitively with separation and everlasting torment. No wonder there are over 38,000 different Christian sects. There is a continual need to be right. After Paul's conversion he said, "*I have become all things to all people. (1 Corinthians 9:22)*

Yet fundamentalist Christians have not done this. They say, "*Believe like me or die.*"

Right or Righteous?

In Chapter Two I wrote of experiencing something I call divine dissatisfaction during a meeting in my home where I sat in the midst of 40 people and declared, "*There has got to be more than this!*"

It was the year 2000 and I was so tired of hearing about another Christian getting cancer, or dying from a horrible disease, or getting divorced or jailed for sexual abuse. Weren't we to be the moral and ethical compass? That day I sat and pounded my fists on my knees in sheer disillusionment of my faltering and flawed religion. My pleas of desperation fell on a few souls who with me bravely nodded their heads, "yes." It was then that I decided to bring in an out of town guest that was known as a religious wrecking ball—who fearlessly slammed into dogma, unrighteousness and corrupt Christian doctrine. I liked him. He was a sort of gangster Christian serving as an Apostle within a radical and growing worldwide Apostolic Christian sect.

One day at the beginning of a series of meetings with this man he made a statement that changed me forever. He said boldly,

> "*For those that think Satan and Lucifer are one and the same, I am here to tell you, THEY ARE NOT. But don't believe me, search for yourself.*"

Incredible lengths and great latitude have been applied to the interpretation of scripture to form dogma that is just plainly and simply, incorrect. He was right. I researched the scriptures and went back to the original language searching and they, Lucifer and Satan, are not the same. In fact Lucifer was not a noun in the original translations as in a *being* rather it was an adjective. The word translated from luciferous (bringing or providing light) and is a reference to the original state of Divinity before its decent into humanity or the world of matter. The word translators say Lucifer is actually he-lel or star, morning star. Morning star is another name for Jesus. I would challenge any disbelieving reader to do the same—search for yourself. Do not just blindly believe what you are told. That is the epitome of laziness—and I should know—I was a lazy believer for decades. Having begun the inquiry into why I believe what I believe, my dogmatic beliefs were tumbling like Humpty Dumpty off of the wall. Some of the best advice I have received to date was; *"search for yourself"*.

...my dogmatic beliefs were tumbling like Humpty Dumpty off of the wall.

Over the next several years I experienced many adjustments in my doctrinal stance along with paranormal or supernatural experiences. I woke up twice with a glowing and glistening being standing near me, unhindered by furniture, floor or ceiling. No words were exchanged, as I lay there propped up on my elbows observing until it faded into my room scape. However, both episodes were harbingers of incredible change in my understanding of spiritual principles. I had been divinely intruded upon during my sleep and my spiritual consciousness it seemed, experienced *adjustment*.

I remember once when I was asleep, I heard my son tell me that he had arrived home after a late night out. I awakened, but before I exited my dream state completely, I motioned to an instructor of sorts who stood near me pointing to some kind of chart or graph, and said that I would be right back. I sat up in bed and responded to my son and then wondered...*where had I just been?* It seemed as though it was some sort of instructional setting. Similar occurrences like that have happened several times before and since.

In 2003 I got very sick. I was diagnosed with a double ear infection, a sinus infection, a bacterial infection in my throat and bronchitis. I felt as if I would surely die. It was as though I was swallowing glass and my whole body throbbed with pain. I remember clearly undergoing a doctrinal shift about the purpose for evil and recalled the teaching about Lucifer and Satan. *Who was Satan then, if not Lucifer?* Standing in the hot shower steam I silently asked for understanding about Satan and one-third of the angels (who according to dogma subsequently turned into demons as they fell from heaven) that the devil supposedly talked into leaving heaven to come to Earth to torment and afflict people. If Satan is not who and what I think he is, then what about demons? What are they? Have we got it all wrong? What are demons?

Then suddenly an impression hit me. From out of nowhere an internal voice spoke that said:

"You are the stars."

What? Stars? I was asking about demons I thought to myself. The voice continued and said, *"Read."* I had thought for a moment that my fever was causing me to hear voices.

I threw a towel on and immediately grabbed my Bible and turned to the book of Revelation Chapter Twelve and read about the one-third of the angels that fell with Satan and to my surprise, I read this:

That the great dragon drew and threw THE THIRD PART of the STARS and cast them to the Earth.

After doing some investigation I saw that the tail of the dragon represents deceit, lies and false prophesy. **The third part of the stars**, not one-third of the angels (or demons) but stars, were drawn through falsehood and cast down or thrown to the earth. Falsehood can be seen as a false sense of identity, when we identify with the world of matter rather than our own authentic nature as Divinity. It was told to Abraham that his descendants would be as numerous as the stars in the sky *(Genesis 26:4)* so people are compared to stars. In considering the third part—not "one-third", I reasoned that we were first and foremost **Divinity**, secondly a **body** and thirdly **soul**, this according to Genesis when God breathed into man and he became a living soul. *The third part—the soul or mind, was drawn out of heavenly places by a false sense of identity.*

The third part—the soul or mind, was drawn out of heavenly places by a false sense of identity.

So you can see that my doctrinal stance began to crumble under the weight of revelatory intrusions. Now what was I going to do? I felt as though my foundation had been built on false identity. Who or what was to blame? After disillusionment had set in I realized I had no one to point the finger at but me. I believed what I had been told rather than searching for answers myself. It is easy to buy into fear and fear-based theology when you are afraid. The frequency of fear was complimentary to what my faith had been based on.

I have had two rather scary ER visits concerning my heart. The first time was in 1994 when a battery of tests was done to see what was wrong—I had bouts of tachycardia and irregular beats. After two weeks of exhaustive testing nothing was found and my heartbeat went into regular rhythm. This happened dozens of times from that time until the next ER visit in 2006. In 2006 I suffered, not for hours, which were now normal, but rather days of an irregular heartbeat where all I could do was lay on the couch. I would feel surges of energy in my body that would bring me to the place of almost blacking out. I finally had my husband take me to the ER after more than 48 hours of irregularity. Once in the ER, I was hooked up to an EKG, but before they could press the start button I felt my heart go into regular rhythm. Again, nothing was found but they sent me for another battery of tests again with the same conclusion—nothing was wrong. After this event in 2006 I continued to experience many episodes of this energy coming over and into me. I can remember lying in bed and my body was moved into a state of extreme discomfort. Lyle was traveling out of town but my sister was visiting from Wisconsin. *I need to go get her to take me to the hospital,* I thought. It was odd though, because I could not say what was wrong with me—I had no specific pain, just extreme discomfort. I heard the internal voice say, "JUST BREATHE."

I lay still and began to take in deep breaths, in and out, while I felt something like mild electrical current flow through my body and after 30-45 minutes I drifted off to sleep. These occurrences happened regularly but with lessening intensity. Finally one night I woke up with the whole bed shaking and vibrating (without quarters!). I awakened Lyle, and asked him if he felt it. Thankfully, he said "yes." Many times I felt absolutely crazy when these odd things happened. That night I thought we might have been having some sort of seismological event in our area. It lasted for several minutes and reoccurred several nights following. Then we travelled to North Carolina and it happened in the Holiday Inn! All right, I thought, *what in the world was happening to us?* After several months of this unusual thing happening, I woke up again, this time the vibration was within my body itself. Again, I awakened Lyle and he felt my vibrating body. He made fun of me the next morning, but he didn't laugh for long because it began happening to him as well. Still, I had no understanding of what was happening to us but I did have a clue. Because along with these unusual happenings came greatly expanded understanding of spiritual things and in particular metaphorical understanding of scriptures. My intuitive abilities were blossoming. We were *evolving.*

I also had a third visitation of a *being* in my room where I awakened the next morning with an understanding of the ego and its place in humanity—some of which you have been reading in this book. I just woke up with an expanded view of a wide variety of spiritual things. It seemed as though my prayers of *"More Lord"* were heard.

I hope that through reading this chapter I have helped stimulate the intuitive channel that will allow for an increase in conscious input from sources other than literalism. We all carry that spark of the Divine within us. It is a veritable and exhaustive library accessible with a 24/7 key. And that "key" is a tone or frequency comprised of courage and non-judgment to challenge traditional thought and belief. This frequency or key fits into and accesses the mysteries found outside of the law, outside of fear, outside of literalism.

Summary Points:

- Divinity has invested the invaluable into the temporal; the eternal Spirit into a mortal frame.

- There have been many "investments" of Divinity into mortality, a little bit at a time so as not to overwhelm the delicate human nervous system.

- Day by day, and millennia after millennia we can see the consciousness of the human being advance and retreat like breath in lungs, retaining what is valuable and expelling the useless. Progress is made in such ways and human consciousness is always on the move, albeit restrained in part by the standards of each passing age.

- In this moment a quantum leap of epic proportion occurs and this leap is perceived as missing in the evolutionary ladder because the creature had moved from animal to human. There is no missing link—it was never there. Somehow the consciousness of the creature experienced a dramatic and immediate upgrade, which produced a new creature.

- We are anointed beings practicing Divinity in a mortal environment.

- Fundamentalist Christianity has willingly placed itself in a dogmatic "time out" where its consciousness has become an oxbow lake in the still waters of literalism.

- Jesus was a revolutionary. He bucked the status quo system of Judaism and he was killed for it. Viewed metaphorically, he sets a pattern for us when we break down the barriers of dogma (unquestioned belief), ritual and ceremony.

- Paraphrasing, Jesus said of his persecutors, "If they did this to me they will do it to you." Those ambassadors that carry this revolutionary message will face the firing squad of religion, just as (Saul) Paul persecuted and killed the followers of Christ, the harbingers of change.

- I felt as though my foundation had been built on false identity. Who or what was to blame? After disillusionment had set in I realized I had no one to point the finger at but me. I believed what I had been told rather than stopping and searching for answers myself.

- It is easy to buy into fear and fear-based theology when you yourself are afraid.

Chapter Eleven

Homosexuality—Exempt from Heaven?

At this time on planet Earth we are being given a wonderful opportunity to step away from judgment and into love and acceptance. As you will see in the chapters ahead, non-judgment along with forgiveness are vital "drivers" that will allow us to transition into the age to come. Throughout our human history we have been given many hurdles to leap, including recent issues like slavery, women's rights, etc.

I want to take some time and explore the possibility of homosexuality as a key template for our blossoming consciousness at this juncture in our human journey. What is it that we need to see in this pattern?

Homosexuality is a hot topic these days with many U.S. States voting on the legalism and legitimacy of same sex marriages. It is a polarizing subject not just in the U.S. but worldwide with the fundamentalist camp rigidly holding a place of traditional marriage by citing scriptures condemning homosexuality. It is a sad thing when souls are told they are not worthy of heaven and deserving of hell because of their sexual orientation. Some have come to such a place of despair that they take their own life. That is a travesty. No human being is unworthy. I bristle at the thought of hate groups present in our news that picket funerals of returning war veterans and homosexuals. Recently, I watched an online video of a couple of individuals on a talk show being interviewed calling homosexuals "fags" and stating that they will go to hell. These two individuals were pastors of a Baptist church. I wished that I had been a part of the audience and had the opportunity to question them myself. They seem to adhere to Old Testament standards of Law and disregard the mission of Christ to *set us free from that Law*. Everything in me wanted to shout at my computer screen the Old Testament scripture about gluttony (they were both overweight). Furthermore, I wanted to ask them if they ate shrimp, or dressed in clothing with blended materials, both things forbidden under the law that they claim to uphold. So many of these issues came to mind and I wanted so badly to tell them of the scripture that says if you place yourself under one law then you are responsible for keeping all of it (over six hundred of them!); an impossibility for perfection according to Jesus. But I have to remember that people will awaken when they have had enough sleep. It is fruitless to try to awaken someone slumbering in egocentric human-hood.

I was speaking at a conference recently and I asked the attendees, *what did Jesus say about Homosexuality?* Silence. I waited and looked around the audience and asked them again, *what did Jesus say about it?* Again, silence, and I said, *that's right. He said nothing.* And there is a reason for that. For Christ, in the pattern and example of an awakened human being, homosexuality was a non-issue. References to it are found in the Old Testament, but Jesus, the revolutionary, was silent on the topic. I don't know about you, but if someone raised his own body from the dead, I think it would be wise to follow that guy. There was and is a good reason for the silence. Jesus condemned no one, yet he was hardest on the religious; those who claimed to have the *right stuff.* Jesus was a reformer. There was reason behind all of the law and it served a purpose during its relevant time frame. But Jesus came to model a path outside of the law. This path is non-judgment.

> *Do not judge, and you will not be judged. Do not condemn, and you will not be condemned. Forgive and you will be forgiven. (Luke 6:37)*

The instructions from Jesus are for those that have *ears to hear.* It can't get any plainer than this. On the transcendent path there is no judgment; there is no condemnation; there is forgiveness. Jesus did not teach the Old Testament law; he transcended it. He did not abolish it; he fulfilled it by following the two commands to Love God and love your neighbor as yourself. To follow the path of Christ you must not judge or condemn and you must forgive. It's that simple. It is LOVE.

Now more than ever there is an awakening people that are following the example set by Christ. This transitioning and transcendent human group comes from all walks of life and out from all religions and the best part of all is they are beginning to declassify themselves, for without judgment there are no labels.

... without judgment there are no labels.

There is a popular teaching in Christianity these days called Inclusion. Inclusion doctrine accepts everyone, sentences no one to everlasting torment and believes all will eventually be saved. Finally an opportunity has arisen for the church at large to step away from judgment and the condemnation of others that may not believe the same as they do. It is a movement gaining momentum albeit at a price. Those that teach inclusion have come under fire for carrying the message by the staunch adherents to fundamentalism. But according to statistics, Christianity is on the decline because the consciousness of the human being has eclipsed systematic religion. It simply will not be restrained any longer. And these same brave souls are beginning to glimpse heaven...within them.

No one is exempt from the arms of the Divine. However, I didn't always believe that. I was very condemning, judgmental and exclusionary—a real pain in the arse. It seemed I felt I had the market cornered on heaven—saying who would get in and who wouldn't. Since then I have questioned, *what exactly is heaven?* Most people have an idea of some place we go to after we die; a place of reward if we do and believe the right things. Nonsense.

As human consciousness ascends, so does the environment we find ourselves within. Heaven begets heaven.

Every dimension needs a driving influence. Heaven is an environment that is created from and through elevated consciousness where we are not entrenched in the world of duality, right, wrong, good and evil, light and dark. It is a state of consciousness that transcends the egocentric realm and functions with love, compassion, allowing and non-judgment. As human consciousness ascends, so does the environment we find ourselves in. *Heaven begets heaven.* It is void of everything so hellish that we find in our present world of duality. There are no tears, no sicknesses, no strife, no war, no abuse, no violence, no disease or death. *It is heaven.* And, we have been programmed to believe that there is a place more awful than our existence. It does not serve me to write of the horror that is present in our world. We all have watched the news and know of the depravity here. Non-belief in who we really are will keep mankind here, in this world where the ego of man, mortality and everything that goes along with it, dominates our consciousness. The ruler in this present reality is called the EGO. Jesus taught us of the kingdom where the Divine within transitions to the throne as the ego willingly steps down to serve the human, *instead of mastering it.*

By design, many homosexuals carry within themselves a very high vibration that is not of this world. These brave souls who live their truth know that they are perfect *just as they are.* Those still affected from the onslaught of condemnation that others heap on them must begin to turn from the conflict and embrace their perfection and their value in and for the human race. In this turning they will remember the purpose for their incarnation.

The energy behind homosexuality is highly evolved and, in part, manifests into unconscious beings, blessed by the immortal order of Melchizedek. (Genesis 14—Look for it—it's in there.) These have willingly come en masse to Earth at this crucial time *on assignment* to *unconsciously reflect* to the judgmental individual their own disqualifying trait, which is, failing to join feminine to masculine, or the human will to the Divine nature within. This non-union of opposites is our own unseen and internal condition that manifests as judgment between good and evil—evidence that the consciousness of the individual is based in duality; the human's willful submission into union with the Divine manifests as non-judgment. Therefore where there is finger pointing and judgment, there is lack of union or oneness and the need for the reflection.

Oh yes, this world provides a rich backdrop made up of every emotional current there is. Our world is a place that is propagated and sustained by lower thought or consciousness with judgment serving as the principal driver. Our judgment propels emotional current through our energy body thereby producing and sustaining our present world of duality. Duality is a world where the human ego flourishes as it recognizes similarities and differences and makes a differentiation between them. It is an environment that is purposeful as it serves the developing mechanism of the human being, that aspect of us, that is able to direct thought and emotion, creating its own world and its own reality. We are just practicing here.

The Earth is a school where the transcending human will learn these three things:

1. We are the creators of our reality—we continually create by our focused thought and emotion.

2. We can create a bridge that will span the gulf between one dimension or age and the next.

3. We are the "saviors" the world is waiting for.

With this magnificent ability to create through judgment we must exercise wisdom. For when we point our fingers at another who we feel falls short of our definition of righteousness, we sentence ourselves to the same judgment. Remember, that is because *the judgment with which we judge another will fall upon our own heads*. And we, loving our judgments and our need to be right, don't get it. If we judge, we will be judged. If we condemn, we are ourselves, condemned. If we do not forgive, we will not transcend the age. The mere fact that we judge between good and evil, sentences us to remain in this dual world and prohibits us from advancing in consciousness. Please don't misunderstand; our judgments have been useful and necessary up until this point in time. But it is now time to transition the age and in order to transition—we must disengage from the behavior (gear) that brought us here.

> *Do not judge, or you too will be judged. For in the same way you judge others, you will be judged, and with the measure you use, it will be measured to you. (Matthew 7:1-2)*

This is why I say that homosexuality is a template. These brave souls agreed to subject themselves to all sorts of familial and societal difficulty and are mirroring to us our own spiritual condition. By simply observing homosexuality in the natural, it is an *in your face* template as human beings that do not produce life via pregnancy within their body. As a human race, we do not enter into union with the Divine by failing to bring our human will to a place of yielding to the Divine and therefore do not produce spiritual life within our body. The human race is the womb and Divinity is the seed giver; without the human race yielding to the Divine, there can be no impregnation to form the Christ.

When we point our fingers at homosexuals, are we not falling under the same judgment when we fail to bring ourselves into union with the Divine?

> ***"Do not judge, or you too will be judged.***
> ***For in the same way you judge others, you***
> ***will be judged, and with the measure you***
> ***use, it will be measured to you."***
> ***(Matthew 7:1-2)***

The surrender of feminine to masculine produces the atmosphere of ascension and will propel us out of dualism and into union or oneness because the TWO become ONE. It is a matter of surrendering our human will to that of the Divine will within, our authentic self. Let us not be so shortsighted as to judge someone who has a different sexual orientation than we do lest we likewise are judged for our own spiritual condition or lack of it. Like the Christ, homosexuality is a non-issue.

Let's look at John, Chapter Eight where the teachers of the law and the Pharisees brought a woman caught in adultery before Jesus stipulating that the law says that she must be stoned. But Jesus said:

> *Let anyone who is without sin cast the first stone. (John 8:7)*

He went on to say that we judge by human standards but that he (the Christ within) judged no one. No one is exempt from "sin" and Jesus was trying to get us to see that even to judge someone is sin.

This is a mystery; to participate in judgment is what sustains the world, as we know it. Jesus was trying to reveal a secret; that judgment in accordance with the law is actually what drives and sustains sin.

Sin is the environment that is created when we are under the control and dominion of our ego.

But let's not stop there. We need to take a deeper look to see what sin actually is. Most think that sin is any number of acts but it is so much more than that. *Actions are only symptoms of an underlying condition.* Duality is SIN. Sin is living according to mortal and limited standards dictated by the ego within man that discerns culturally between right and wrong. WE ALL LIVE IN SIN. Sin is the environment that is created when we are under the control and dominion of our ego. It is said there is no remission [of sin] without the shedding of blood *(Matthew 26:28)*— metaphorically, *the shedding of blood* is death to the life of self (ego) so that we might be raised to a new life free from the environment of sin.

Here is a mystery:

The Apostle Paul writes this:

The sting of death is sin; **and the strength of sin is the law.**
(1 Corinthians 15:56)

Paul, the overseer of the fledgling seed of Divinity within the human was given the task to bridge the gap between the ages as the human migrated out from the law and into grace. The fundamentalist does not perceive that it is he who wanders in the wilderness of human and egocentric judgment and is sentenced to death (mortality). We die in the wilderness, just like the pattern set in the Old Testament story because of our unbelief in this very principle. Those not so entrenched in religion step out from judgment easily, while the fundamentalists find it difficult to let go of their need to be "right."

The message of Jesus was to reveal that we have been set free from the LAW. Now that it has finished its education in duality, consciousness is ready for a shift. Why is it then that we still judge against what we perceive is good and evil according to our viewpoint of good and evil? We are addicted to duality. The EGO is a duality maniac and needs to partake from the tree of knowing good and evil, and more than that, it needs to feel "right."

I recently shared this with the young man who does my hair—he is gay and has had so much hurt in his life, especially from religious folks. He told me of those that told him he was exempt from heaven.

I said,

"Let's look at the scriptures regarding homosexuality through the eyes of metaphor—that men should not lie with men is a pattern in nature, but metaphorically it is an exhortation to bring together masculine and feminine energies (humanity + Divinity) and the ensuing punishment of damnation (sentenced to mortality, that is, hell, or a state of immanent death) if you do not."

I went on to say that,

"The literal translation however, was a necessary enforcement of the law in its time; after all, the planet needed to be populated. But we really miss the mark if we do not investigate further to understand what the male and female represent metaphorically. It isn't about sex, it is about union between the human and the Divine. Sex is just a physical pattern so that by it we can 'see' what is unseen. The feminine must willingly yield to the masculine. Divinity needs a framework or womb in which to incubate the life giving seed that is given. Without this union, there can be no manifestation of Christ. No one is exempt from incubating and birthing the Christ."

I know that he did not understand everything I said in that moment, but there was an unconscious part of him that did. Right there in the busy salon he buckled over gasping for breath and breathing in deeply. Then the tears came. I knew that he had been loosed of the pain from religious judgment that had been placed on him since he was a little boy.

In transcendence and awakening we will see the masculine and feminine roles expressed in union, both working together within one body. After all, there is no male or female in the age to come—we will be Emanuel, formatted to renew life within the body as masculine seeds life into the feminine time and time again, quickening mortal to immortal and sustaining that state of being, eternally. This is at the heart of the mortal becoming immortal.

We are being called out of our era of judgment and limitation. We must grasp this template concerning homosexuality in order to move past judgment and into the all-inclusive love that is the very fabric of the age to come. Furthermore we must understand the nature of evil and why it is a necessary component for our education.

There are various cultural identifications of evil throughout the world. Here is an exhortation from Jesus not to resist evil:

> *But I say to you resist not evil: but whosoever shall smite you on your right cheek, turn to him the other also. (Matthew 5:39)*

We do not understand this exhortation. The fundamentalist does not want to follow this Jesus. If they did, there would not be continual finger pointing and condemnation of others. The ego is the one that separates one from another and nation against nation. It is this corporeal ego that must have a "cross" experience so that it might rise again as a new creature.

Then there is the paradoxical scripture that says resist the devil.

> *Resist the devil and he will flee from you. (James 4:7)*

The devil we are to resist is the driving force of the ego within. It is this devil that appears externally until the creature understands that it is a reflection of man's own internal nature. As humans, we need an external foe to affix blame. It is hard for the ego to come to the realization that it is in fact the adversary of the burgeoning Christ that is being birthed within. It is hard for us to see that we, our collective egocentric nature, are the Anti-Christ.

We all must come to the point of our own crucifixion where the life of ego as master of the mind and body relinquishes its role in favor of the one that becomes servant of the Divine. Remember, the ego in submission is the metaphorical donkey as it bears the Son of Man—YOU to Calvary. It is likewise the white steed of the Book of Revelation as it undergoes transformation from master of earthly burdens to valiant servant of the risen Christ (Christ in you, the hope of glory).

It is through this path, and this path only, that the body is raised from mortal to immortal. This is what it means to be "saved." Jesus modeled this path and stated that it was the only way to the Father—the progenitor, the source of all. It is not a reward for raising a hand or walking an aisle and is not preferential to Christians. This is a hard thing for Christians to understand—that their religion is not the panacea that they espouse—and yet another indicator of the ego at large within our consciousness as it finds expression in duality and rightness.

Let's take a further look at the sexes; Paul states the following message and instruction:

Women should remain silent in the churches. They are not allowed to speak, but must be in submission, as the law says. If they want to inquire about something, they should ask their own husbands at home; for it is disgraceful for a woman to speak in the church. (1 Corinthians 14:34-35)

And then he speaks this:

Husbands, love your wives, just as Christ loved the church and gave himself up for her to make her holy, cleansing her by the washing with water through the word, and to present her to himself as a radiant church, without stain or wrinkle or any other blemish, but holy and blameless. In this same way, husbands ought to love their wives as their own bodies. He who loves his wife loves himself. After all, no one ever hated their own body, but they feed and care for their body, just as Christ does the church—for we are members of his body. For this reason a man will leave his father and mother and be united to his wife, and the two

*will become one flesh. This is a profound mystery—but I am
talking about Christ and the church. (Ephesians 5:25-32)*

It is clear to me that Paul spoke mysteriously through metaphor
in regards to male and female, men and women in their roles. Not
only was he giving practical, cultural instruction (albeit sexist for
today's standards) but he was also speaking an internal mystery that
was yet to be made manifest. Once we understand the symbolism of
men and women we understand that women (the womb-man or the
collective mind within all of humanity) should be silent in church
(not a building but the dwelling place of Divinity within) and if there
is questioning we are to ask the husband (Divinity within).

Within these two scriptural passages lies profound instruction
given to the collective egocentric mind within all of us. This female
counterpart must "submit" to her husband, the Divine energy within.
It is not about God favoring one sex over another, it is about the love
story and the romance as it develops between the Divine and the
human. Once this message passed its cultural and timely relevance, it
is so silly to take such a passage literally. The Bible is a book of
metaphors that if we take the time to "see" we will gain
immeasurable understanding of all that is and all that will be.

Paul was given the charge of the fledgling seed of the Divine that
the human had been inoculated with. During the growth of this seed
there was still great need for rules and regulations and law, for the
seed in its infancy is not yet dominant within the human—the
collective ego still is. But there comes a time in everyone's personal
journey and evolution that we must put away things of childhood so
that we may go on to perfection. Jesus modeled perfection and as
such DID NOT JUDGE or live according to the law in thought or
deed. So why do we? There is need of our religious institutions to
enforce a structure of spiritual confinement much like the Catholic
Priests centuries ago that discouraged parishioners from reading the
scriptures. This was done in order to self-propagate—the church
needed to maintain attendance and DEPENDENCE. Such is not the
model from Jesus within scripture. There were no large buildings
with huge salaries that had to be maintained.

Recently, a rather large church in our area built another huge structure and I had to comment on it in our local newspaper's opinion section. In the article I cited the division within the Christian community with each church vying for attendees and I asked this question:

"If the Apostle Paul wrote to the church at large in our city, which one would get the letter?" Perplexingly what the Christian church has in common with other competing denominations is division.

If the Apostle Paul wrote to the church at large in our city, which one would get the letter?

I think we have come to a point in time where we need to take a serious look at what Jesus taught separately from other scriptures so that we can grasp his message without having other texts cloud the issues. Jesus was clearly teaching us about a different place in consciousness, a whole different age that he occupied, and a place that he said we could attain. What he taught flew in the face of the people of the day so it was quite natural that the egocentric religious adherents sought to kill him. Jesus manifested the future condition of humanity out of time itself. The past most often resists the new.

It is not uncommon for books and information such as this to come under the ax of the dogmatic patrol and the heresy hunters. The ego wants and needs to feel in control and *right*. When dogma is challenged, the ego ruffles its feathers much like a black bird readying for a fight. But the time for such control wanes as the light of a new day dawns. Remember, masses of people are exiting such religious institutions in favor of the freedom found outside the restrictive structures we call "church" to the tune of six thousand members a day—two million per year. The numbers are staggering.

Jesus was asked about a woman married several times—whose wife would she be in the afterlife? He replied:

The people of this age marry and are given in marriage. But those who are considered worthy of taking part in the age to come and in the resurrection from the dead will neither marry nor be given in marriage. (Luke 20:34-35)

In another scripture it is said that *there is neither male nor female in Christ (Galatians 3:28).* Clearly, a focus on homosexual marriage is an indication of attention to matters other than the age to come or kingdom. But Jesus said, *"Seek ye first the Kingdom." (Luke 12:31)*

To me homosexuality is a non-issue. Acceptance and love are the drivers that will propel us to enter the age to come.

I read this statement recently on Facebook:

"To tell a child that if they don't believe something they will be sent to hell for eternity to be tortured in inconceivable ways is ideological blackmail. This is a form of child abuse, and it perpetuates a broken and delusional society." Facebook.com/wakeupfromreligion

We will be hearing a lot more about religious abuse—it is an up and coming phrase fit for a society that is blossoming beyond the constraints of fundamentalism. Like Moses said, *"Let my people go!"* It is time to challenge the systems of egocentricity and begin to love, truly love and accept one another.

In closing, these brave individuals offer to us an opportunity to come away from judgment, their lives as a rendering of sorts that reflect to us, that tell of our own disqualification when we fail to cease from our judgments, surrender as a bride to a groom, our ego to Divinity.

Summary Points:

- Regarding homosexuality: Now more than ever there needs to be a voice of reason that will challenge limiting dogma by discovering the metaphorical teachings of scripture and what they mean for us today.

- Inclusion doctrine accepts everyone and sentences no one to everlasting torment.

- No one is exempt from the arms of the Divine.

- Heaven is a state of consciousness that transcends the egocentric realm and functions with love, compassion, allowing and non-judgment as principal drivers.

- Judgment is the principal driver of our present world of duality.

- Duality is a place where the human ego flourishes as it recognizes similarities and differences and makes a differentiation between them.

- Duality is an environment that is purposeful as it serves the developing mechanism of the human being, that aspect of us that is able to direct thought and emotion and thereby creating its own world, its own reality, learns.

- The Earth is a school where we ultimately learn these three things:

  1. We are the creators of our reality.
  2. We can create a bridge that will transcend this reality as we are destined to build the bridge between one age and the next.
  3. We are the "saviors" the world is waiting for.

- WE ALL LIVE IN SIN. Sin is not an action, it is an environment.

- Too often the Christian does not perceive that it is he who wanders in the wilderness of human and egocentric judgment and will be sentenced to death in the wilderness, just like the pattern set in the Old Testament story because of their unbelief in this very principle.

- The Apostle Paul, the overseer of the fledgling seed of Divinity within the human was given the task to bridge the gap between the ages as the human migrated out from the law and into grace.

- Those not so entrenched in religion step out from judgment easily, while the Christian and other fundamentalists find it difficult to let go of their need to be "right."

- The devil we are to resist is the force that drives the ego within ourselves—the one who sits as the son of perdition making himself to be like God.

- It is this devil that appears externally until the creature understands that the Biblical accounts show a reflection of man's own internal nature.

- As humans, we need an external foe to affix blame.

- It is hard for the ego to come to the realization that it is in fact the adversary of the burgeoning Christ that is being birthed within.

- We, our collective egocentric nature within, are the Anti-Christ.

- We all must come to the point of our own crucifixion where our humanity intersects our Divinity and the life of ego as master of the mind and body relinquishes its role in favor as one that becomes servant of the Divine.

- We will be hearing a lot more about religious abuse—it is an up and coming phrase fit for a society that is blossoming beyond the constraints of fundamentalism.

Phase Four

Embracing Your Divinity

Chapter Twelve

The Necessity of Forgiveness

I have heard it said that *"unforgiveness is like drinking poison and hoping the other person gets sick"*. Also, *"whosoever angers you, controls you"* and *"forgiveness is a gift we give ourselves"*. Forgiveness has great value, eternal value sometimes beyond human comprehension. The benefits of forgiveness affect the physical, emotional and mental bodies and not least of all it benefits your spiritual body. So why do we hang on to injustices as if they were a lifeline when they are more like an anchor strapped to our ankle? Ah...the ego. The sense of self we derive when we continually see ourselves as separate from one another provides an opportune canvas for us to paint our backdrop of pain. Oh, and what a memory for recall the ego has—photographic in fact—albeit tainted with self-perception. Each painful memory moves the stroke of the brush and adds to the canvas until the beauty of the portrait is marred. The brush becomes a blade disfiguring the life, as the painter becomes the painted, splashed with the blackness of betrayal, abuse and rejection. The original sketching with weakness of voice speaks through the bloody mire,

> *You are not a victim; you are a participant. There is no human suffering in vain. All suffering produces something of great value in the Earth.*

The gift of suffering is not recognized or appreciated until we release our need to be justified. Suffering produces change.

Forgiveness is a gift we give ourselves.

The ego judges between good and evil, right and wrong, justice and injustice and most always will seek compensation for perceived wrongdoings. The ego seeks for and dines on judgment, validation and consensus. When we really grasp the role that the ego was created to play, we will understand that it is only doing its job. Until enlightenment dawns, we remain in a state of duality and mortality continuing to feel and reap the effects of life and death through, and because of, unforgiveness.

There is one parable that Jesus taught where he states that if we do not forgive we are given over to prison to be tormented *(Matthew 18:34)*. Since most of us have harbored unforgiveness and we were not physically put in a penitentiary where we were tormented, then what is this prison? The prison is duality and the torment is the continuing cycle of mortal life and death, never entering into what we have been promised, immortality.

In Chapter Three I told you of my son's traumatic accident where he lost his left arm and leg and the voice I heard in the emergency room telling me *he chose this* and that so had I. If this is true, then how can we harbor unforgiveness against any perpetrator when we are the ones that have chosen our life lessons? Somewhere along the line there must be a shift in our consciousness that moves us out from our victimhood and into the role of an active participant. This shift will expand our viewpoint and ultimately allow us to see our purpose for life here in the school of planet Earth. That shift comes with forgiveness.

Here is a parable that in all my years within Christianity I had never heard explained:

He also said to his disciples:

> *There was a certain rich man who had a steward, and an accusation was brought to him that this man was squandering his wealth. So he called him and said to him, "what is this I hear about you? Give an account of your stewardship, for you can no longer be steward." Then the steward said within himself, "what shall I do? For my master is taking the stewardship away from me. I cannot dig; I am ashamed to beg. I have resolved what to do, that when I am put out of the stewardship, they may receive me into their houses." So he called every one of his master's debtors to him, and said to the first, "How much do you owe my master?" And he said, "A hundred measures of oil." So*

he said to him, "Take your bill, and sit down quickly and write fifty." Then he said to another, "And how much do you owe?" So he said, "A hundred measures of wheat." And he said to him, "Take your bill, and write eighty." So the master commended the unjust steward because he had dealt shrewdly. For the sons of this world are more shrewd in their generation than the sons of light. "And I say to you, make friends for yourselves by unrighteous mammon, that when you fail, they may receive you into an everlasting home." (Luke 16:1-9)

If we look at the rich man and the steward as templates/metaphors for the Divine and the ego both dwelling within one body, then we can see the message in this often overlooked and not understood parable from Jesus. The ego is in charge of the master's business and is being chastised and warned that it is squandering wealth and is being called to account. The ego is warned that Divinity will not keep the ego employed as steward of his business. The steward/ego then determines slyly that he must slash the amount of receivables owed to his employer in order to make friends with them so that when he is put out of employment as steward of the business and unemployable he will have a place to stay. Then in a surprising turn of events the rich man/Divinity returns and praises the steward for reducing the receivables. It is acknowledged that the steward behaved shrewdly in this world and had won for himself friends that will welcome him into their *eternal dwellings* when he is released from his position. Among other things, this tells me two very important keys: One, the ego will be released from being master of the body and all its workings in consciousness and two, the ego will be welcomed into eternity.

Could it be that *reducing receivables* is actually metaphorical language for the forgiveness of debt, as in *forgive us our debt as we forgive our debtors* from the Lord's Prayer? Is this *"squandering of wealth"* the priceless resource of the gift of forgiveness? Once the forgiving of debt is accomplished and the original role of the ego "fails" it is welcomed into an "everlasting home" or into immortality. The ego has a central role in the age to come.

I hope to encourage you today to stop judging the events of your life as good or evil as this is a prerequisite for awakening. When we begin the cessation of judgment regarding various injustices committed by others, only then are we poised to forgive the whole realm of duality recognizing that we have received a wondrous and necessary education through it all. And in this act of forgiving debt we are behaving shrewdly and wisely.

> *I hope to encourage you today to stop judging the events of your life as good or evil as this is a prerequisite for awakening.*

As youngsters we cannot really appreciate our education within the school systems until long after we have graduated. It is the same here on planet Earth. The Earth—and the environment of duality—is purposeful and necessary for the Spark of Divinity invested in humanity as well as for the ego within man. The Earth school provides the necessary immersion into mortality for the purpose of cultivating the pearl of Christ consciousness within the human. Divinity needs a mechanism; a vehicle that can focus thought and emotion and that vehicle is the mind of the human with the ego as its steering wheel, the prime navigational device.

All along, this masterful plan has been about cultivating a servant. Divinity as unexpressed consciousness in materiality (sheer energy) needed a vessel through which to occupy space in the material world. Once it found a means to penetrate the material form (the biology of human DNA), it needed to foster necessary relational capacity, courting a spouse, a willing helpmate, and a partner through whom the immaterial could inhabit and find expression in the material world. This beautiful and perfect helpmate is the human being. It is YOU.

This present age has allowed for the exercising of our emotions to discern good and evil, something that we will see is necessary as we enter into the age to come. This parable also reveals another key piece of information: the ego is welcomed into "eternal shelters" or into eternity. The ego has been through the Earth school having learned the ultimate task of forgiveness. Upon graduation, the mechanism that can focus thought and emotion (the ego) transitions with the body into the age to come. Both thought and emotion will take on new form and function in the coming age.

As we begin the process of forgiveness we will see that all along we have been creating our reality with thought, emotion and judgment; that is, deeming something to be good or evil, light or dark. Reality is like a loom, and when we judge something utilizing the appropriate emotional value (i.e. grief, sorrow, anger etc.) it is akin to taking a shuttle and weaving it through the threads on a loom. When we pronounce judgment it is like pulling down the battening arm of the loom to force the weave into place amongst the threads in the fabric.

So often we feel put upon, that things happen to us, rather than for us and it is at this juncture in thought that we begin to reinforce reality as victims of circumstances. It is vital for our progression through consciousness that we hit the pause button and re-evaluate our life's experiences. Once we grasp that we are molding our reality and begin to change the way we think, the things we think about are changed and reality will follow suit. Our perspective changes and we become the happy, buoyant beings we are created to be. In time, reality shifts in accordance with how we think about it.

You are the higher authority that can override your ego.

I don't mean to sound trite or that this is an easy process. This is like overriding hard-wired circuitry. Sometimes while standing in a checkout line the cashier will reach a point where a transaction freezes and needs to call for assistance. The manager appears, types in a password, and presses keys to override the transaction. The computer is no longer stuck because a higher authority has unlocked it. You are the higher authority that can override your ego. You are Divinity having a temporary mortal experience.

The ego is not wrong for pronouncing judgments, it is doing what it has been designed and created to do. The ego is supposed to recognize similarities and differences and to judge between them. This is what drives this present reality, the dimension of duality or knowing good from evil. It is what creates and sustains our environment. The ego "eats" from the tree of the knowledge of good and evil every moment of every day and it is supposed to do so. It bears the fruit of duality. HOWEVER, and it is a big HOWEVER, if we wish to transition the age, then it becomes absolutely necessary to disengage the gear that drives this present reality. It will not be business as usual that propels humanity to shift into a different age. Enter the passwords. Those words are "courage", "allowing", "acceptance", "forgiveness" and "non-judgment". Forgive and accept your life's course. It is what it is. And the key that you will have in your hands is the frequency or tone that comes from peace—peace that comes from allowing and accepting your life's circumstances. Courage, peace, allowing, acceptance and forgiveness are dissonant tones for this present age of conflict. Those that practice such things are considered "out of touch" with reality and indeed, they are. The frequency of fear dissolves in the face of these passwords.

> *For God so loved the world, that He gave His only begotten Son, that whoever believes in Him shall not perish, but have eternal life. For God did not send the Son into the world to judge the world, but that the world might be saved through Him. (John 3:16-17)*

You are that Son.

Summary Points:

- I have heard it said that unforgiveness is like drinking poison and hoping the other person gets sick.
- It has also been said that whosoever angers you, controls you.
- Forgiveness is a gift we give ourselves.
- When we begin the cessation of judgment regarding various injustices committed by others, only then are we are poised to forgive the whole realm of duality recognizing that we have received a wondrous and necessary education through it all.

- Divinity *needs* a mechanism, a vehicle that can focus thought and emotion and that vehicle is the mind of the human with the ego as its steering wheel.

- All along, this masterful plan has been about cultivating a servant. Divinity as unexpressed consciousness in materiality (sheer energy) needed a vessel through which to occupy space in the material worlds.

- Reality is like a loom, and when we judge something utilizing the appropriate emotional value (i.e. grief, sorrow, anger etc.) it is like threading a shuttle and weaving it through the threads on a loom.

- When we pronounce judgment it is like pulling down the battening arm of the loom to force the weave into place amongst the former threads in the fabric.

- So often we feel put upon, that things happen to us, rather than for us and it is at this juncture in thought that we begin to reinforce reality as victims of circumstances.

- It is vital for our progression through consciousness that we hit the pause button and re-evaluate our life's experiences. Once we grasp that we are molding our reality and begin to change the way we think, the things we think about are changed and reality will follow suit.

- If we wish to transition the age, then it becomes absolutely necessary to disengage the gear that drives this present reality.

  For God so loved the world, that He gave His only begotten Son, that whoever believes in Him shall not perish, but have eternal life. For God did not send the Son into the world to judge the world, but that the world might be saved through Him (John 3:16-17)

You are that Son.

Chapter Thirteen

Non-judgment—The Driver of Unfolding Consciousness and the Use of Emotion

As mentioned in the previous chapter, judgment is the driver of this passing age. As we get ready to shift gears in consciousness, we must learn how to *put the clutch in* and stop judging. Judgment keeps us embroiled in the process of threading the fabric within the mortal reality loom. If we wish to ascend, we must disengage. Like the saying, *"Don't throw good money after bad"*, disengagement means to stop throwing your valuable emotional currency at the bad circumstances of life. Judgment is absolutely creative. When the human imbued with Divinity judges a thing as good or evil, it reinforces the nature of the thing being judged and sustains reality, as we know it.

These two great metaphors help relay the concept that will allow for the eventual cessation of the present age of duality: the clutch and the loom.

Disengagement means to stop throwing your valuable emotional currency at the bad circumstances of life.

The clutch: A pedal that is pressed to disengage the drive train moving it to a neutral position. It is from this action that the next higher (or lower gear) can be engaged.

The Loom: A mechanism used to create a woven fabric. The cessation of threading the weave stops the formation of the fabric.

Metaphorically, I am suggesting that the cessation of judging good from evil will cease OUR PART in driving and creating the fabric of this age.

This emotional current is dispensed like payment from our energy body to create the fabric of our lives.

When we judge something we are spending a type of vibrational currency in the form of emotional energy. This emotional current is dispensed like payment from our energy body to create the fabric of our lives. The typical human creates by default; not realizing its ability to create reality using focused thought and emotion.

If Divinity resides in our body, and it does, then we have the ability to create. The human will run amok creating endless conflict as it focuses thought and emotion on turmoil, creating more of what it does not want just by thinking and providing the appropriate emotional value to the object of its focus. Paul understood this principle and encouraged us here:

Take captive every thought to the obedience of Christ. (2 Corinthians 10:5)

Jesus modeled the path of Christ and encouraged us to think of things "above" and not below.

For as he thinks in his heart, so is he. (Proverbs 23:7)

This is the essence of the *Law of Attraction.* Pushing the clutch in disengages the transmission and if we are to ascend into the next age, we must shift into neutral and eventually into a higher gear. Judgment is the driving creative force of this present age, and it is here that the human learns that it is creating its environment, albeit by default and largely unconscious.

I mentioned the "time gap" in Chapter Three—there is an expanse of time between our focused thought and emotion and the ultimate manifestation of our request. Presently we are largely unaware that we are creating because of this gap in time. However that gap is narrowing with each human that awakens and that begins to create consciously.

We must begin to be socially responsible for the energy we bring to any given circumstance. This is the beginning of the death, or crucifixion of the egocentric self. We must learn to restrict the release of our emotions and eventually to master them. Ego surrenders its role as the driving force to this dimension and ultimately surrenders or submits to this higher self—this the crucifixion of our ego-centric life.

We must begin to be socially responsible for the energy we bring to any given circumstance.

As I stated earlier, a prerequisite for this *death to self* is the understanding of the nature of evil in our dual world. I have vast experience as an exorcist within the church system. Now, instead of fighting against evil I understand the necessity of dualism or the knowledge of good and evil and the role it plays in our developing consciousness. I also understand that what we resist persists. It always bothered me when we would have such great difficulty setting some folks free from demonic oppression and possession. I used to say—*this is not how Jesus did it!* Jesus modeled for us the cessation of the need for evil and simply cast it out and away with little to no effort. His consciousness was well educated as a multi-dimensional being and he knew the mechanics that drive this dimension. Non-resistance is key.

Evil is like ballast that keeps the ship of humanity in part submerged in dense consciousness. While we are in this age this ballast is absolutely necessary to maintain our equilibrium in duality. I have come to see that the knowledge of good and evil yields to humanity a full spectrum of light and dark threads that provide the necessary contrast to form this beautiful tapestry called mortal life. As we learned in Chapter Three, all things are made beautiful in their own time. Non-judgment, forgiveness and understanding the purpose for duality will bring all of our karmic cycles to an end. Jesus said:

> *But if I drive out demons by the finger of God, then the kingdom of God has come upon you. (Luke 11:20)*

This tells me that, as we get ready to transition into the kingdom that the ballast of evil will be released from creation with ease.

Evil is like ballast that keeps the ship of humanity in part submerged in dense consciousness.

Jesus came to deliver us from evil so that human consciousness could be buoyant once again. Forgiveness is the key that will release the ballast from the ship. The ballast anchors us in mortality and duality by the sheer focus of our thought and emotion upon the various injustices we deem to be evil. In order to transition this mortal age, we must understand that judgment directs the creative force of emotions.

As I travel and speak on this subject there are many voices that object to the notion of not judging evil. The only thing I can say is that if you are called to judge evil in our world *then judge.* If you are called to help transition the age by understanding the purpose for it, *then stop judging.* There are those that are called to work with what is breaking down (this passing age) and there are those that are called to work with what is breaking through (the age to come).

If you are called to help transition the age by understanding the purpose for it, then stop judging.

Jesus patterned the proper use of emotions to enforce His creative will in the scriptural account of raising Lazarus from the dead:

> *Then when Mary was come where Jesus was, and saw him, she fell down at his feet, saying unto him, Lord, if you had been here, my brother would have not died. When Jesus saw her weeping, and the Jews also weeping which came with her, he groaned in the Spirit, and was troubled, And said, where have you laid him? They said unto him, Lord, come and see. Jesus wept. Then said the Jews behold how*

174

*he loved him! And some of them said, could not this man,
which opened the eyes of the blind, have caused that even
this man should not have died?*

*Jesus therefore again groaning in himself came to the
grave. It was a cave, and a stone lay upon it. Jesus said,
Take away the stone. Martha, the sister of him that was
dead, said to him, Lord, by this time he stinks: for he has
been dead four days. Jesus said to her, I said to you that if
thou would believe, you will see the glory of God? Then
they took away the stone from the place where the dead was
laid. And Jesus lifted up his eyes, and said, Father, I thank
you that you have heard me. And I knew that you hear me
always: but because of the people which stand by I said it,
that they may believe that you have sent me. And when he
had spoken, he cried with a loud voice, Lazarus, come
forth. And he that was dead came forth, bound hand and
foot with grave clothes. (John 11:32-44)*

As the story goes, Jesus is summoned to come to Lazarus, as he
lies ill. Jesus delays his journey there at least four days (Lazarus was
only two miles away) and they wonder about his lack of urgency to
tend to a man that he loved. Jesus, it seemed, was not moved by
human urgency or emotion. He took his time getting there and
Lazarus died waiting for him to arrive.

Upon arrival to the grave of Lazarus we see that Jesus wept and
groaned loudly in his Spirit. He then thanked his Father (the creative
principle within) and Lazarus was raised from the dead. It is
interesting to note that Jesus groaned within himself and then
thanked the "Father" for hearing him, and states that he [the Father]
always hears him.

This groan was the movement of his energy body, calling upon
the rich experience of grief to raise the dead. Through this example
we see that Jesus did not allow his emotional judgment to move him;
rather he moved his emotions and raised Lazarus from the dead. This
is key! Disengaging from judgment (or to cease being moved or

pulled by our emotions into action by judgment) is paramount to our spiritual advancement.

> ## *We see that Jesus did not allow his emotional judgment to move him; rather he moved his emotions and raised Lazarus from the dead.*

You might recall in Chapter Three, the account of Christian's accident where my husband laid on Christian's lifeless body, gathered him up in his arms and wailed. Christian came back to us. There is something magnificent that we are learning as human beings imbued with Christ. The things Christ did, we will also do; and greater. He is a pattern for our own ascension.

Very truly I tell you, whoever believes in me will do the works I have been doing, and they will do even greater things than these, because I am going to the Father. (John 14:12)

Summary Points:

- As we get ready to shift gears in consciousness, we must learn how to put the clutch in and stop judging.
- Disengagement means to stop throwing your valuable emotional currency at the bad circumstances of life.
- The cessation of judging good from evil will cease OUR PART in driving and creating the fabric of this age.
- The typical human creates by default, not grasping or realizing that it has great ability to create reality using focused thought and emotion.
- There is an expanse of time between our thought and focused emotion and the manifestation of our request.
- We must learn to restrict the release of our emotions and eventually to master them.
- A prerequisite for this death to self is the understanding of the nature of evil in our dual world.

- Jesus did not allow his emotions to move him; rather he moved his emotions.
- The things Christ did we will also do; and greater.

Chapter Fourteen

Inversion, Divine Alchemy and The Resurrection of the Dead

I was speaking with a friend recently that had been my spiritual mentor for most of the 1990's. Nell is heavily involved in Christian ministry, traveling, speaking and teaching all over the world. She is a bit of an anomaly; not your normal Christian, prophesying and having all sorts of supernatural experiences. She is rather accurate with her predictions and has always been a wealth of spiritual information. Nell was my *go to* person whenever I had a question and I could sit and listen to her teach for hours on end. She was and still is a fascinating woman.

Back in the 1990's she talked a lot about something called *Divine Inversion* where she would say unusual things like, *"What is out is in and what is up is down"* and the like. Sometimes when she spoke of these mysterious things, it was a little hard to follow what she was saying. And, maybe she didn't understand everything either but she was tapping into something otherworldly, and was faithful to say what she saw. I know that when I receive intuited information it oftentimes takes a while to process and understand what is being *received*. The idea of *divine inversion* never left me, and I often wondered what it meant.

Nell has boundless energy and bright blue eyes that will pierce right though you along with a smile that lights up a room. She visits me on occasion and on this day we were busy as bees chatting and buzzing about the latest spiritual revelation.

As we talked, I could tell that my evolving spiritual stance was throwing up a few red flags in her although she has always been accepting and loving. I spoke of *"divine inversion"* saying that I felt like I was beginning to understand it. I said,

"Everything is inside of us! Jesus said the kingdom is within you. Hell is not a place but is a state of consciousness and Satan—well Satan is our egocentric nature. It is the creative component within that is an ADVERSARY to our Divinity. As such it creates and maintains our mortal world. The Old Testament tells of the ego's journey that needed rules, regulations and boundaries until the time when the Christ seed was deposited into Mary and grew. And metaphorically we are Mary! This is the new story or the NEW TESTAMENT! We are the ones that were overshadowed by the Divine and impregnated with Christ! This Christ is being birthed in us, through us, as us—It is not outside of us, it is inside of us! The manger is within! The Garden of Gethsemane is within! The temptation in the wilderness is within our consciousness as the ego tempts us to follow it! The disciples are the twelve different aspects of our consciousness that surround the Christ! Judas is the aspect of our self that delivers us up to death time and time again. Luke is our healer! Peter is the aspect that can hear the voice of the father. John is closer than a brother. We are being built into a multidimensional habitation of the Divine just like it says in the Book of Revelation. Our multidimensional body is the New Jerusalem that descends out of 'heaven.' And heaven is a higher state of consciousness just like the 'upper room' where we meet Christ. It's all INSIDE OF US!!! It is not external! This is the Divine Inversion! Consciously, reality as I have known it, is inverting!"

I blurted this all out to her in a matter of seconds. She stared blankly at me for a moment or two and then slowly, deliberately and authoritatively she said:

"Barbara, you cannot say there is no hell for I have been there. You cannot say there is no devil for I have stood before him."

Like I said, Nell has experienced a wide variety of unusual spiritual phenomena and I did not want to discredit any of it. It was all valid and useful in its time.

I had been leaning in speaking to her and so I straightened and replied,

"These things will appear externally as long as you need them to."

I felt a strong measure of knowing and confidence in my statement. This is a woman I deeply respect and it seemed as though with this reply that I no longer occupied the same conscious space with her that I had previously. Clearly my thinking was no longer the same as hers. I had made a significant shift in my understanding. I had experienced *divine inversion.*

In Chapter Two I said,

"For human consciousness to evolve it needs to see an externalization of spiritual principles."

But if we fail to see the patterns, the allegory and the symbolism, we may miss the coming of Christ...within.

Presently we have an external God, a devil, Heaven, Hell and Christ and we have a whole lot of historical, linear events. The ego sees and perceives these historical and conceptual stories externally until we can learn to intuit by them, that which is unseen. There will come a time when we will automatically cease to see Biblical events as literal although they may have happened in our historical accounts. But if we fail to see the patterns, the allegory and the symbolism, we may miss the coming of Christ... *within.* The human must experience inversion in consciousness to see clearly. It is like stepping out of the proverbial and literal forest to see the metaphorical trees. By looking at the scripture metaphorically, allegorically and symbolically the Bible presents to us what lies within. Remember in Chapter Four, the scripture speaking of Old Testament events even calls itself examples and allegory:

These things happened to them as examples for you upon whom the end of the age has come. (1 Corinthians 10:11)

The end of the age is the transition period from our dualism (eating from the tree of the knowledge of good and evil).

> *For it is written that Abraham had two sons, one by the bondwoman and one by the free woman. But the son by the bondwoman was born according to the flesh, and the son by the freewoman through the promise. This is allegorically speaking, for these [women] are two covenants: one [proceeding] from Mount Sinai bearing children who are to be slaves; she is Hagar. Now this Hagar is Mount Sinai in Arabia and corresponds to the present Jerusalem, for she is in slavery with her children. But the Jerusalem above is free; she is our mother. (Galatians 4:22-26)*

These two women also represent our procreative abilities as it relates to creating finitely via the ego (Hagar) or eternally by Divinity (Sarah). To invert these and other scriptures is a process in consciousness where we do not see historical applications, but rather we see that they are archetypical, expressed within cultural stories down through millennia, the mystery of our incarnation, our falling asleep within the dream of materiality and of our ultimate awakening.

Throughout this book I have mentioned awakening, transitioning, ascending, morphing and changing. Jesus spoke of things like the age to come and the Kingdom. He was not like other people because he could perform paranormal feats that would astound those about him.

Deepak Chopra in his eye-opening book, *The Third Jesus* talks about three concepts of Jesus. He says:

> *"First there is the historical Jesus, the man who lived more than two thousand years ago and whose teachings are the foundation of Christian theology and thought.*
>
> *Next there is Jesus the Son of God, who has come to embody an institutional religion with specific dogma, priesthood, and devout believers.*

And finally there is the third Jesus, the cosmic Christ, the spiritual guide whose teaching embraces all humanity, not just the church built in his name."

One might say we can view Jesus historically, religiously or mystically.

As far as the historical Jesus goes, there are those who hold the opinion that Jesus was a myth, and that he never actually lived. Here is a scripture that speaks of Jesus coming in the "flesh."

This is how you can recognize the Spirit of God: Every Spirit that acknowledges that Jesus Christ has come in the flesh is from God, but every Spirit that does not acknowledge Jesus is not from God. This is the Spirit of the antichrist, which you have heard is coming and even now is already in the world. (1 John 4:2-3)

It seems that there was, even back then, some disagreement as to whether Jesus actually came in the flesh. But might this scripture also be used for those staunch adherents to literalism that denies that Christ is within our flesh *now*? Let's not get so hung up on the historical Jesus that we fail to see and embrace the message found within his teachings. Now as for Jesus, the Son of God who embodies an institutional religion I might suggest to some that they rethink their ideology and the pattern of the serpent on the pole. Jesus compared himself to this pattern *(John 3:14)* and in the end, the God of the Old Testament became very angry at their worship of this serpent on the pole. What was to bring healing as they "looked to it" became the object of their idolatrous worship and the snake and pole were destroyed in his wrath. If the serpent on the pole was a symbol of healing and the idolatrous worship of it, its demise—then how does that apply to the rampant disease within our biology? Are we being destroyed?

Again, as I stated in Chapter Five let me expound even further when Christianity points to this scripture as evidence that Jesus is to be worshipped:

Therefore God exalted him to the highest place and gave him the name that is above every name, that at the name of

Jesus every knee should bow, in heaven and on earth and under the earth, and every tongue acknowledge that Jesus Christ is Lord, to the glory of God the Father. (Philippians 2:9-11)

As I interpret this scripture with an inverted view, the Christ within me is acknowledged as "Lord" of my body. In other words, I acknowledge that Divinity within is my authentic identity. It, the Christ, has a greater measure of authority within my body, mind and soul. Having experienced the process of *death to self*, my egocentric nature, or *"knee"*, bows in humility and servitude to the Christ within, the aspect of me that has come into union with the Divine, as a bride yields to her groom. This "worship" (humility and servitude to the Christ within) will cause the egocentric nature to transform the creature as energy ascends the spinal column (the serpent rising on the pole). As ego gives way to Divinity, it brings life immortal to the body. External worship pales in comparison to becoming that which you behold and Jesus embodied this archetype, the bridegroom—not just the groom, but also the bridegroom as he experienced this wedding between the mind of man and Divinity within. This brought about resurrection.

The acknowledgement of the Christ within, resurrecting the body from mortal to immortal is the metaphoric *serpent rising on the pole* that brings healing when we "look to it" (understand and follow the pattern). We see that worshipping something externally was considered idolatrous and brought about their ultimate destruction. Those that worshipped the pole in the wilderness were destroyed along with the serpent on the pole. The serpent on the pole is a metaphor for an egocentric being that is undergoing transformation through ascendancy. They stopped looking to the pole as a pattern for their ultimate healing and *worshipped the image instead*. Because of this, a new generation was birthed in the wilderness and the old generation *perished there*.

In Chapter Eight, I mentioned this scripture:

Therefore leaving the principles of the doctrine of Christ, let us go on unto perfection; not laying again the foundation of repentance from dead works, and of faith toward God, Of the doctrine of baptisms, and of laying on of hands, and of resurrection of the dead, and of eternal judgment. And this will we do, if God permit. (Hebrews 6:1-3)

Let's look at the admonition in this scripture to leave *"the principle of faith toward God"*. While on vacation in Hawaii we had rented a Harley Davidson motorcycle and rode all over the Island of Oahu. I love riding on the back of a motorcycle. My mind goes blank as there is nothing for me to do other than to take in the beauty around me—it's like a form of meditation. As we rode through the rainforest I was thinking about this scripture in Hebrews as I had been stumped by it for weeks. Why I asked, would we be told to leave behind *faith toward God*? The wind had a gentle mist about it, tingling my skin as we rode, and I heard that voice within say this:

*"The key to understanding the message behind this scripture lies in the word **toward** for it implies directionality outward from you. You are misapplying your faith to an external position."*

I came to understand this voice as the "I AM" within—hearing *I am within you, as you.*

Again, our externalization of God was necessary until the Divine penetrated the framework of man. Now our worship should be an act of becoming: Becoming fearless; Becoming non-judgmental; Becoming love; Embodying forgiveness; Loving the Divine. This is the cosmic Christ that Mr. Chopra spoke of. It is the unique amalgamation of God and man that is uniquely Christ. Are we God? No. We are not the totality of God. I heard it said that if God were the ocean, we are a glass dipped in the ocean. Is the ocean within the glass? Yes. Are we the totality of the ocean? No. We are over 7 billion individual expressions of the Divine yet we are all ONE.

The human frame has given animation to the Divine in the material world. We are the helpmate. We are Eve.

The human frame has given animation to the Divine in the material world. We are the helpmate. We are Eve.

Divine Alchemy

Alchemy is defined as: *1: a medieval chemical science and speculative philosophy aiming to achieve the transmutation of the base metals into gold, the discovery of a universal cure for disease, and the discovery of a means of indefinitely prolonging life 2: a power or process of transforming something common into something special 3: an inexplicable or mysterious transmuting.*

Something very special is occurring on our planet. As we awaken spiritually to our identity as Divinity, coupled with humanity, we are experiencing change within our physical bodies. I speak to many people that are having odd things happen to them as they migrate out from dualism or judging between good and evil. The list is long and diverse but suffice it to say that a leap in our physical evolutionary process is happening. Many express difficulty within the electronics of their body—heartbeat, thyroid, adrenals etc. Heart palpitations are very symptomatic of the changes taking place within us. As the vibration of our consciousness changes, our body follows suit. The vibration of our consciousness elevates daily as we choose the path of fearlessness, love, forgiveness and non-judgment.

The world of dualism produces an energy spectrum every time someone judges between good and evil, dispensing valuable emotional currency into the environment. As we continue with the awakening process, the range of vibration on the planet rises along with us. It is like changing the environment within a terrarium, when the energy changes, the growth within the terrarium changes as well. In short, our mortal bodies are experiencing a sort of transmutation process as we migrate into the next age in consciousness. We are experiencing a type of *Divine Alchemy.*

I declare to you, brothers and sisters, that flesh and blood cannot inherit the kingdom of God, nor does the perishable inherit the imperishable. Listen, I tell you a mystery: We will not all sleep, but we will all be changed—in a moment, in the twinkling of an eye, at the last trumpet. For the trumpet will sound, the dead will be raised imperishable, and we will be changed. For the perishable must clothe itself with the imperishable, and the mortal with immortality. When the perishable has been clothed with the imperishable, and the mortal with immortality, then the saying that is written will come true: 'Death has been swallowed up in victory.' (1 Corinthians 15:50-54)

This scripture tells me that as the kingdom is manifested (a realm where the Divine within rules the material domain of the body) that something other than flesh and blood bodies *will enter it*. The Kingdom represents the immortal environment of Divinity. It says we shall not all sleep (die) but we will be changed. The word moment is *atomo* and it means uncut and indivisible. Do you see the word atom? We will be changed within our atoms as Divinity and humanity experience union. The twinkling of an eye speaks to enlightenment as duality gives way to singularity, when the two shall become one. The last trumpet is the seventh chakra as it releases the sound of ascension.

Resurrection

Resurrection from the dead is not what we think it is. We see images of graves busting open and zombie-like forms regaining life and vitality when we think about resurrection, but it may not look like we think. The ever-increasing vibration of our planet, called the Schumann Resonance, is a harbinger of sorts that reflects from us this advent of change. This change in frequency reflects what is happening within our physical bodies as this seed of Divinity grows up within our flesh and blood, bringing change in modicum over the centuries. We are now becoming conscious participants elevating our own vibratory range by the willful departure of lower emotional values—all by overcoming fear and through the cessation of judgment. Can you imagine the peace that comes when we do not focus on the evil in our world? Withdrawing from fear-based judgment and entering into peace and joy will do more for our health and wellbeing than all of the doctors on the planet put together.

**Slowly, like a cocooned caterpillar, the
human within the organism of skin is
changing form from the inside out; a new
creation is being built.**

We carry with us, in our vibrational escrow, this increasing vibratory range into every incarnation. We live multiple lives during which karmic hindrances are hurdled and debt forgiven; we evolve our malleable framework, and are in a process of becoming. This is the process of Divine Alchemy, moving us from the base human consciousness into that of the golden ages to come. It is cyclical lasting approximately 26,000 years; we are within this cycle and seizing the opportunity to enter into this alchemic process, while the Earth readies itself for its seasonal harvest of Christ consciousness.

Slowly, like a cocooned caterpillar, the human within the organism of skin is changing form from the inside out; a new creation is being built. Just as the water breaks within the birth sac, likewise human consciousness "breaks" and the god-men are birthed, sloughing off the consciousness of mortal man, breathing the ether of heavenly domains. This new synergy that is both celestial and terrestrial is emerging, and the crop whose seed was planted during the cyclical Age of Pisces is being harvested.

**Just as the water breaks within the birth sac,
likewise human consciousness "breaks" and
the god-men are birthed, sloughing off the
consciousness of mortal man, breathing the
ether of heavenly domains.**

As this evolutionary leap in consciousness occurs, our bodies reflect these changes within our electromagnetic and physiological makeup. Symptoms of ascension abound. I have personally experienced many of these mysterious symptoms—everything from severe heart palpitations to my body vibrating in bed at night to skeletal changes. I have gone to the doctor to have these symptoms checked to rule out anything that might need attention but sometimes there is just no explaining these odd occurrences except to say, *"shift happens."*

I hope I have brought a level of comfort to the reader as we leave behind egocentric modes of operation, our bodies will experience the process of manifesting resurrection and ascension. We become living tuning forks that help relieve *"negative vibrational ballast"* from ourselves and also from those that no longer need to navigate the waters of human consciousness through duality. We will set the "tone" for the age to come.

Summary Points:

- Regarding Heaven, Hell, Satan, God, "These things will appear externally as long as you need them to."
- For human consciousness to evolve it needs to see an externalization of spiritual principles.
- The ego sees and perceives these historical and conceptual stories externally until we can learn to intuit by them, that which is unseen.
- There will come a time when we will automatically cease to see Biblical events as literal although they may have happened in our planet's history. But if we fail to see the patterns, the allegory and the symbolism, we may miss the coming of Christ within.
- The human must experience inversion in consciousness to see clearly.
- From *The Third Jesus* Deepak Chopra writes:

  "First there is the historical Jesus, the man who lived more than two thousand years ago and whose teachings are the foundation of Christian theology and thought.

  Next there is Jesus the Son of God, who has come to embody an institutional religion with specific dogma, priesthood, and devout believers.

  And finally there is the third Jesus, the cosmic Christ, the spiritual guide whose teaching embraces all humanity, not just the church built in his name."

189

- One might say we can view Jesus historically, religiously or mystically.

- I came to understand the "I AM" within—hearing *I am within you, as you.*

- The human frame has given animation to the Divine in the material world. We are the helpmate. We are Eve.

- We will be changed within our atoms as Divinity and humanity experience union. The twinkling of an eye speaks to enlightenment as duality gives way to singularity, when the two shall become one.

- The last trumpet is the 7th chakra as it releases the sound of ascension.

- The ever-increasing vibration of our planet, called the Schumann Resonance, is a harbinger of sorts that reflects from us the advent of change.

- Withdrawing from fear-based judgment and entering into peace and joy will do more for our health and wellbeing than all of the doctors on the planet put together.

- As karmic hindrances are hurdled and debt forgiven, we are evolving our malleable framework, and are in a process of becoming.

- Slowly, like a cocooned caterpillar, the human within the organism of skin is changing form from the inside out; a new creation is being built.

- Just as the water breaks within the birth sac, likewise human consciousness "breaks" and the god-men are birthed, sloughing the consciousness of mortal man, breathing the ether of heavenly domains.

- As this evolutionary leap in consciousness occurs, our bodies reflect these changes within our electromagnetic and physiological makeup. Symptoms of ascension abound.

Chapter Fifteen

The Melchizedek Priesthood—Your Multidimensional Self

Following our discussion about Divine Inversion, Nell told me that the things I was speaking of would be commonplace in forty years. Previously, Nell had prophesied over me saying that I would suffer abuse from those who would not, or could not, embrace the revelatory information I was bringing to them. I would be considered controversial and Nell said, *"Controversy will follow you wherever you go, get used to it."* She also said I would suffer abuse from those within the church and would be the subject of accusation, slander and rumor—all of which has come true.

Throughout my life, what others thought about me was important and I was a fearful child and adult, always second guessing myself and lacking in confidence. When I re-entered the church arena in my thirties it seemed as though I had found my niche. I was a teacher, and placed in positions of leadership. When I began to question traditional Christian thought and doctrines, I stepped onto a slippery slope and ended up alienating many friends and church associates. Try as I may, many could not hear or understand what I was teaching. And so I offer these things to you. Controversial? Yes. Challenging? Yes. Fascinating? Absolutely!

To summarize the previous chapters:

- When you begin to evolve spiritually it is wise to leave the old system rather than to try to convert those still within it. They will remain in restriction as long as they need to.

- Leaving the old system is consciousness no longer subject to fear.

- You must move from victim to participant understanding that your pre-incarnate self has chosen your path, knowing what you need as an individual personality to grow and evolve.

- New consciousness is flexible and expansive and not limited to one set of dogmatic beliefs. It is expedient for your growth to let go of the things that no longer serve you.

- You must let go of the Christian idea of Jesus as he has been constructed with intolerance, fear and judgment; the antithesis of what is spoken of him in the New Testament.

- Learn and understand the word "Christ."

- Begin to see scripture metaphorically and as such see that the human race is the Virgin that has been penetrated by the Divine and pulsates with the holy thing within waiting the time of birth.

- Understand that the previously held understanding of baptism is but a shadow of the truth; that Divinity has laid down its immortal state to be swallowed up of death in the realm of mortality and time.

- See that Divinity has and is coming in your flesh and blood with moments of Divine Intrusion.

- The energy behind homosexuality is highly evolved and, in part, manifests into unconscious beings, blessed by the immortal order of Melchizedek. These have willingly come en masse to Earth at this crucial time *on assignment* to *unconsciously reflect* to the judgmental individual, their own disqualifying trait, which is, failing to join feminine to masculine, or the human will to the Divine nature within. This non-union of opposites is our own unseen and internal condition that manifests as judgment between good and evil—evidence that the consciousness of the individual is based in duality. The human's willful submission into union with the Divine manifests as non-judgment. Therefore where there is finger pointing and judgment, there is lack of union or oneness and the need for the reflection. You must forgive not just circumstances and people but your whole divergence into time, space and mortality. Earth is your classroom.

- To progress into the age to come, non-judgment is essential in that the fabric that sustains this present age is no longer created on the loom of mortal reality.

- You will see that all of reality is expressing externally what is internal and unseen by the ego. Divine inversion is taking place as we awaken to our identity as Divinity, and as Christ within the manger of humanity.

- You are a multi-dimensional being that has chosen the Earth as your classroom. As you awaken, your energetic make-up begins to change and you become capable of navigating through multiple dimensions...again.

Much of what I know about the Melchizedek order is intuited. It comes from the same source that revealed that Jesus was the Christ to Simon as referenced in Chapter Seven. You must take responsibility for your own intuited knowledge and not take my word for it. You are encouraged to drink from your own well rather than someone else's. You must develop your own listening abilities.

If we look even deeper into Matthew 16 we will see a surprising turn of events. As we now know, the name Simon, which means listening, was changed to Peter, which means stone or rock. Simon listened to that still small and revelatory voice from within and we are told that it is upon this "rock" or revealed knowledge that we are being established as the church, that is us, as multi-dimensional habitats capable of hearing the voice of the Divine within. The church isn't what we think it is. If we continue reading Matthew 16 we see that surprisingly Jesus calls Peter "Satan":

> *When Jesus came into the coasts of Caesarea Philippi, he asked his disciples, saying, "Whom do men say that I the Son of man am?" And they said, "Some say that thou art John the Baptist: some, Elias; and others, Jeremiah, or of the prophets. He said unto them, "But whom say ye that I am?" And Simon Peter answered and said, "Thou art the Christ, the Son of the living God." And Jesus answered and said unto him, "Blessed art thou, Simon Barjona: for flesh and blood hath not revealed it unto thee, but my Father, which is in heaven." From that time Jesus began to show*

*his disciples that he must go to Jerusalem and suffer many things from the elders and chief priests and scribes, and be killed, and on the third day be raised. And Peter took him aside and began to rebuke him, saying, "Far be it from you, Lord! This shall never happen to you." But he turned and said to Peter, **"Get behind me, Satan! You are a hindrance to me. For you are not setting your mind on the things of God, but on the things of man."** (Matthew 16:13-23)*

You see Peter was listening to the voice of the human ego that is set upon the things of man—on selfishness that has its own idea of things. Peter was telling the Christ that he wouldn't have to die. Metaphorically, we tell ourselves that we don't have to surrender our human will up to death. This is similar to the serpent in the Garden of Eden that she wouldn't die if she ate of the apple. That is not the pattern that Jesus needed to display and so Peter was sternly corrected by identifying the voice of the adversary (Satan) within.

We have within us two wells from which to draw consciousness. From one well comes egocentric human reasoning and intellect and from the other Divinity, Intuition or Source consciousness. Peter drew from the well of Divinity (the Father/Spirit or source within) and spoke things that were not learned from anyone, and so do we. Peter also drew from the well of human consciousness, and so do we.

So we have an adversary to Divinity within us. This adversary is Satan. Just like there is not a little Jesus dwelling inside of us there is not a Satan with horns and a pitchfork in there either. Satan is what is expressed in us and through us when we drink from the well of our own limited humanity called the ego.

Satan is what is expressed in us and through us when we drink from the well of our own limited humanity called the ego.

Humankind anthropomorphizes Satan, as man needs to see an adversary in form outside of himself. We have given Satan an external form rather than understanding that it is our own egocentric nature within. Satan is the serpent in the tree that is within the sophisticated circuitry of human consciousness. Herein lies the ego. Satan is said to have "stood" before the Lord and alongside man in the book of *Job 2 and Zechariah 3*. The three: the Lord, man and Satan are inseparable for they reside within the same being. It was this adversary that met with Jesus in the "wilderness" (egocentric consciousness) tempting him with earthly wealth. We can see this adversary separately but metaphorically we see that it is part of our multidimensional self and not in form separate from us, and as such, not something to be afraid of.

Satan is the serpent in the tree that is, within the sophisticated circuitry of human consciousness. Herein lies the ego.

Jesus predicted this fall of "Satan" from an elevated place in our consciousness when he said this:

> *He replied, "I saw Satan fall like lightning from heaven. I have given you authority to trample on snakes and scorpions and to overcome all the power of the enemy; nothing will harm you." (Luke 10:18-19)*

Heaven is within you. As we awaken, this adversary is falling from this elevated position within our own consciousness. The adversarial nature of our own ego is being "dethroned."

We were taught in fundamentalism of a being outside of ourselves setting himself up to be God, called the *"Son of Perdition."*

> *Now we beseech you, brethren, by the coming of our Lord Jesus Christ, and by our gathering together unto him, That ye be not soon shaken in mind, or be troubled, neither by Spirit, nor by word, nor by letter as from us, as that the day of Christ is at hand. Let no man deceive you by any means: for that day shall not come, except there come a falling away first, and that man of sin be revealed, **the son of perdition;** Who opposes and exalts himself above all that is*

called God, or that is worshipped; so that he as God sits in the temple of God, showing himself that he is God. (2 Thessalonians 2:1-4)

This *man of sin* and *Son of perdition* is none other than the fearful and powerful ego within man. It is this *"falling away"* where the ego falls from its lofty position in our consciousness and consumed with the coming of the Christ—again, an internal happening. When the ego is "large and in charge" the human drinks from a cup of strong delusion.

It is this self-willed human that needs a "cross" experience where his life of egocentricity comes to an end in favor of the surrendered servant. This servant nature sees humanity in need of a savior and humbles itself bearing the human frame to the cross along with the Christ nature that in turn raises the form to a new creation—from mortal to immortal. At this crucifixion, Divinity within us is activated into service.

But if the Spirit of him that raised up Jesus from the dead dwell in you, he that raised up Christ from the dead shall also quicken (make alive) your mortal bodies by his Spirit that dwells in you. (Romans 8:11) [Emphasis mine]

The subject of this chapter is Melchizedek and we know from the limited scriptural references that Melchizedek was considered immortal and without mother or father. I am not sure this means the order was never born of flesh and blood, egg and sperm like we have been or if they have successfully transitioned from mortal to immortal as we have been given to do. I tend to embrace the latter. The Melchizedek order, once they transition out from their human-hood, is considered *born from above* or *born of Spirit*. They are eternally living vibrational links or bridges in consciousness that connect dimensional levels—levels that we are to advance into, and to occupy consciously. They have put on immortality. And we are charged with doing the same.

For this corruptible must put on incorruption, and this mortal must put on immortality. (1 Corinthians 15:53)

Each level of consciousness produces an atmosphere and the level we presently occupy is where the human learns through and about the currency of emotions by discerning and judging events. Unfortunately, we are most adept at learning through the events that bring about pain and suffering.

> *Though he were a Son, yet learned he obedience by the things which he suffered; And being made perfect, he became the author of eternal salvation unto all them that obey him; Called of God an high priest after the order of Melchizedek. (Hebrews 5:8-10)*

This knowledge we accrue comes from a tree that we are told not to eat from lest we become as gods knowing good from evil. It is a warning to the immortal creature that if he chooses to partake in this classroom that he will enter into time itself and become mortal with a statute of limitations on his individual lifespan(s) of up to one hundred and twenty years *(Genesis 6)*. Eating from this tree does indeed produce god-hood as that creative impetus of duality will now reside within the human frame—creating the realm of mortality and all that it entails by employing focused thought fueled with emotion. Then it is within this life of futility that we must learn to bring the life of self, the ego, willfully to a position of death so that it might serve the Divine in its resurrection. It is our cross.

This eating from the tree introduces the creature to mortality through the establishment of time. We are given this superb classroom of Earth from which to learn how to feel emotional values and to discriminate between them. We are gods, celestial and terrestrial learning to navigate through the waters of dense human consciousness. It is sort of like taking a Spanish immersion course where the non-Spanish speaking student travels to and lives in Mexico where his temporary family will speak only Spanish to him—he learns quickly mastering the language. So are we, this Spark of Divinity, immersed into human consciousness learning the language of emotions by the immersion into duality consciousness. Thought, fueled by our emotion, sets in motion our creative potential.

The following information, primarily regarding the Melchizedek Order, is presented for your consideration. Please read slowly letting each thought marinate a little before moving on to the next point allowing your intuitive mind to be stimulated:

- The Melchizedek Priest is multi-dimensional (can traverse at least twelve dimensions).
- There are twelve disciples of the Christ each one representing a different dimensional level.
- Christ is within you.
- Christ is your immortal reality and identity as your humanity yields to your Divinity.
- There are thirteen aspects to our consciousness, one that is physical.
- The twelve disciples surround the Christ in other dimensional levels of consciousness.
- Metaphorically, these twelve disciples are aspects of our developing and expanding consciousness. One is our betrayer (Judas) a part of our self that delivers us up to death time and time again. One is Luke, our healer. One is John that is closer than a brother. One is Peter that hears directly from source itself, etc.
- These twelve gather around and join the Christ in the upper room.
- The upper room is our elevated and developing Christ consciousness where the twelve meet.
- The twelve tribes of Israel are metaphors for our multi-dimensional self.
- Joseph is the one of twelve brothers sold into slavery in Egypt (egocentric life) in order to save all of his brothers from catastrophic drought. You have been sold into the slavery of ego so that you might save all twelve aspects of yourself.
- Drought is lack of water—water represents consciousness.
- Metaphoric templates are found throughout the Old and New Testament and speak of our developing multidimensionality.

Remember Joseph's coat of many colors, tones, aura and the twelve stones on the priest's ephod.

- The twelve levels (disciples) to the "New Jerusalem" are metaphors for our developing consciousness that will reflect a new man, a god-man that has abilities beyond what we see in our limited two-stranded DNA (duality consciousness) and metaphorically establishes the notion of "levels."

- There are twelve notes or tones to an octave; each tribe, each disciple, each level, each aspect has its own unique quality. There are thirteen tones or keys in an octave (if you count the repeating "C"). Each tone or key adds to the richness of the frequency found in our octave. These keys are given to us and are the "keys" to the kingdom that Jesus gave to us (Matthew 16:19).

- The Melchizedek order functions with all tones in its vibrational makeup. Melchizedek priests have earned the right to be physical upon demand. They have mastered all dimensional levels within our octave and some of them are from beyond it.

- These priests provide guidance and assistance here on the Earth in the form of messengers that have agreed to come to sound a vibrational key for us to resonate with, and to help us with our awakening and ascension processes.

- This vibrational key is somewhat higher than what is typical for our limited third dimensional bodies, and will help propel us toward and build a bridge through the vibrational gap that exists between dimensional levels.

- You have heard the saying, "as above, so below," and just like there is a gap between our intellect and intuitive mind, it is reflective of the gap "above" and between the dimensional boundaries.

- This order of immortals called Melchizedek Priests has adopted bodies and walk among us.

- In Genesis 14 there is an offering spoken of that was given to an immortal being called Melchizedek by Abram in the form of a "tithe."

- Metaphorically, the tithe is a people group within the "loins of Abraham".
- A tithe is roughly ten percent of something deemed valuable that is given to the Priesthood for their service to humanity.
- Priests offer themselves in servitude as a mediator between God and man.
- A Melchizedek Priest acts in the same capacity however they offer the service of their vibrational escrow within their energy field to help reconcile the gap between dimensional levels.
- The Melchizedek frequency is a suitable vibration that can occupy the gap between dimensions much like a bridge stands over water and between landmasses.

The first time Melchizedek shows up in the Bible is in Genesis 14. In this passage it speaks of a war that Abram gets involved in after some family members of his are taken captive. Abram is victorious and recovers his relatives, goods and others that had been taken captive from Sodom and Gomorrah. Melchizedek meets and blesses Abram bringing him *bread and wine*. Melchizedek blesses everything Abram has in his possession—this includes the people he rescued, and all of the goods taken as spoils of war. Abram in return gives a tithe that is, a tenth of *everything*. This is where the concept of tithing—giving ten percent of our income to the church.

Included within this tithe was a tenth of *everything Abram had in his possession* including those people from Sodom and Gomorrah and the seed within his loins that is, *a people yet to be born*. I say this because in another scripture it says this:

> *For this Melchizedek, king of Salem, priest of the most high God, who met Abraham returning from the slaughter of the kings, and blessed him; To whom also Abraham gave a tenth part of all; first being by interpretation King of righteousness, and after that also King of Salem, which is, King of peace; Without father, without mother, without descent, having neither beginning of days, nor end of life; but made like unto the Son of God; abides a priest continually.*

> *Now consider how great this man was, unto whom even the*
> *patriarch Abraham (Abram) gave the tenth of the spoils.*
> *And verily they that are of the sons of Levi, who receive the*
> *office of the priesthood, have a commandment to take tithes*
> *of the people according to the law, that is, of their brethren,*
> *though they come out of the loins of Abraham: But he*
> *whose descent is not counted from them received tithes of*
> *Abraham, and blessed him that had the promises. And*
> *without all contradiction the less is blessed of the better.*
> *And here men that die receive tithes; but there he receives*
> *them, of whom it is witnessed that he lives. And as I may so*
> *say, Levi also, who receives tithes, paid tithes in Abraham.*
> *For he was yet in the loins of his father, when Melchizedek*
> *met him. (Hebrews 7:1-10)*

Levi, a priest was in the loins of his father Abram when Abram gave Melchizedek a tenth of all *in his possession*. This tells me that ten percent or a "tithe" of Abrams *seed* was given over to Melchizedek as well. This means that a tithe of humanity that descended from Abram will be given to the service of the Melchizedek Priesthood, an order of immortal beings, a priesthood taken from among mortal men.

This Priesthood bears within their biological frame a higher order of energy that is multi-dimensional and capable of bridging the gap between dimensional boundaries. This tithe offering comes in the form of biology—a body for this potent energy to occupy.

This Priesthood bears within a biological frame a higher order of energy that is multi-dimensional and capable of bridging the gap between dimensional boundaries.

A Melchizedek Priest has already made it through the earth school and returns offering himself as a vibrational bridge between the dimensional levels for man's consciousness to navigate upon and through. When this type of energy occupies a human body, it becomes a beacon or a resonator of sorts that sets a vibrational standard for blossoming consciousness. That standard is love, which carries a high sound standard and easily overcomes fear, a low sound standard. This resonance emits a signal much like a bird to a flower. The chirping of a bird causes flowers to bloom and to yield to the pollination processes. The energy sounding from within a Melchizedek priest causes our consciousness to blossom. These "priests" are here by the millions.

I might compare Melchizedek Priests to the inflatable balloons used to right sunken ships. They are loaded dice walking among us, vibrating like tuning forks to help align our resonance out from fear (the standard for third dimensional reality) to that of love, which comprises the bridge from one age to the next. We have been stuck in the vibration of fear for a long time. As fear gives way to love, we will see giant shifts in human consciousness. This is what the year 2012 represented, a giant leap in consciousness unlike the world has seen in prior shifts. This is undeniably the *biggest* shift we have seen since the inspiration (in-Spirit) that brought us modern man. This shift will propel us toward incredible advances in our physiological makeup as well as within our environment. A new creation is about to be birthed in and through the earth, in and through you.

You have a multidimensional aspect to your vibrational makeup. You are and will be in a state of becoming, blossoming as you progress into your god-hood. I feel many will object to this statement but Jesus is the one that confirmed our Divinity. In this passage in John, the religious order was trying to find a reason to stone him:

I give them eternal life, and they shall never perish; no one will snatch them out of my hand. My Father, who has given them to me, is greater than all; no one can snatch them out of my Father's hand. I and the Father are one." Again his Jewish opponents picked up stones to stone him, but Jesus said to them, "I have shown you many good works from the Father. For which of these do you stone me?" "We are not stoning you for any good work," they replied, "but for blasphemy, because you, a mere man, claim to be God." Jesus answered them, "Is it not written in your Law, 'I have said you are 'gods?' if he called them 'gods,' to whom the word of God came—and Scripture cannot be set aside—

what about the one whom the Father set apart as his very own and sent into the world? Why then do you accuse me of blasphemy because I said, 'I am God's Son'? Do not believe me unless I do the works of my Father. But if I do them, even though you do not believe me, believe the works, that you may know and understand that the Father is in me, and I in the Father." Again they tried to seize him, but he escaped their grasp. (John 10:28-39)

When we begin to talk about our Divinity the religious order of the day gets very nervous.

When we begin to talk about our Divinity the religious order of the day gets very nervous. Within Christian fundamentalism we are told repeatedly how bad we are; sinners in need of a savior. But Jesus came to show us a different way. That way is to drink from a different well, the well of consciousness that reveals to us, our Divinity. Are we human and not gods? Yes. Are we gods and not human? Yes. WE ARE GOD-MEN. And this whole grand experiment is to bring the limited human consciousness to a place where it drinks from another well of being, our Divine nature. In the meantime, the religious order seeks to silence those that claim Divinity.

Whereby are given unto us exceeding great and precious promises: that by these ye might be partakers of the divine nature, having escaped the corruption that is in the world through lust. (2 Peter 1: 4)

We will partake of this divine nature not after we die and go to heaven as Christian dogma claims but we will partake of it while we are in the world. Jesus said he was the firstborn of many brothers and we are his kin. It is not about getting arrogant but it is about embracing our superior mind within and leaving the lust of the ego that always seeks to know something, anything outside of itself. It is not about putting ourselves on a pedestal; it is about serving all from our Divine capacity within.

Jesus is a pattern of Divinity within humankind for the lost sheep Israel *(Matthew 15:24)*. Israel itself is a blend from many cultures expressed to the Jews. IS (Isis the wife of Osiris), RA (the Egyptian Sun God) and EL (the Hebrew Elohim) or IS-RA-EL. All of our cultural stories and myths have within them common threads telling the same TRUTH. *We are gods.* We are Divinity invested into humanity. And we are awakening.

We are Divinity invested into humanity. And we are awakening.

Similar to the ancient practice of Japanese females who have their feet bound to keep them small it is the job of the religious orders of our world to restrain Divinity consciousness. Religion tries to bind our blossoming consciousness with fear. Religion seeks to know through the intellect that which cannot be known to it. Jesus was hardest on the religious order, like a hard nut that needs cracking; Divinity is encased within the ego and needs release. The Christ is the rock that we need to fall upon for our ultimate deliverance. It is offensive to the ego.

As it is written: "See, I lay in Zion a stone that causes people to stumble and a rock that makes them fall, and the one who believes in him will never be put to shame." (Romans 9:33)

Just as with Jesus, the religious order sought to kill him when he spoke of his Divinity, the same will happen to us as Jesus said it would. But if we continue to walk the same path of forgiveness, fearlessness and non-judgment, we will become what we behold.

Beloved, now are we the sons of God, and it doth not yet appear what we shall be: but we know that, when he shall appear, we shall be like him; for we shall see him as he is. (1 John 3:2)

This appearing is Christ within you.

I hope the reader is encouraged to find a place of peace knowing that you are loved and accepted no matter what; that nothing can separate you from the love of God. Indeed you are endowed with the frequency of the Divine. Most importantly, I hope you will know that we have not been left as orphans here on planet Earth. There is abundant help in the form of messengers and they are all around us, cheering us on to finish the (human) race.

Summary Points:

- We have within us two wells from which to draw consciousness. From one well comes human reasoning and intellect and from the other Divinity or Source consciousness.

- Our dream state is a very powerful time of receiving from beyond human reason or intellect.

- Melchizedek Priests are eternally living vibrational links or bridges in consciousness that connect dimensional levels—levels that we are to advance to, and to occupy consciously.

- Each level of consciousness produces an atmosphere and the level we presently occupy is where the human learns about the currency of emotions through the discerning and judgment of events.

- Then it is within this life that we must learn to bring the ego willfully to a position of death so that it might serve the Divine in its resurrection. It is our cross.

- This eating from the tree introduces the creature to mortality through the establishment of time.

- We are gods, celestial and terrestrial learning to navigate through the waters of dense human consciousness.

- Christ is your immortal reality and identity as your humanity yields to your Divinity.

- The upper room is our elevated and developing Christ consciousness.

- The Melchizedek frequency is a suitable vibration that stands between dimensions much like a bridge stands over water and between land masses.

- A Melchizedek Priest has already made it through the earth school and returns offering himself as a vibrational bridge between the dimensional levels for man's consciousness to navigate upon and through.

- WE ARE GOD-MEN.
- It is the job of the religious orders of our world to restrain Divinity consciousness.

Beloved, now are we the sons of God, and it doth not yet appear what we shall be: but we know that, when he shall appear, we shall be like him; for we shall see him as he is. (1 John 3:2)

This appearing is Christ within you.

Epilogue

The Earth has been incubating the Christ seed within humanity for thousands of years. This seed is growing and bearing fruit that comes from maturity. We are beginning to change the way we think and perceive reality.

> *As many as I love, I rebuke and chasten: be zealous therefore, and repent. Behold, I stand at the door, and knock: if any man hears my voice, and opens the door, I will come in to him, and will sup with him, and he with me. (Revelation 3:19-20)*

To repent simply means to change the way that you think. The door is the way into to the egocentric and serpent-like mind within your consciousness. By allowing the Divine within access to walk through the portal it will find for itself the *bride* and *union will occur.* This bride is the womb of creation, a necessary helpmate, the mechanism through which thought and emotion are focused to create reality. The "lightning" of Divinity will flash from the eastern (intuitive) hemisphere of the brain to the western (intellect) hemisphere and the Earth will see the manifestation of the Christ within man.

You are the Son that has been sent to save the world. You are a unique amalgamation of the Divine and man. You must believe that you are so much more than a human—you are the manifestation of Christ in the Earth and through your belief, the world will be saved. Being "saved" is not about escaping the wrath of hell by raising your hand, walking an aisle and accepting Jesus into your heart. *It is believing that the Divine is already, within.*

Acknowledgements

First and foremost to Lyle — I love you more than words can say. You are my champion, my hero and the love of my life. Thank you for all of your support through the years and through the tears. You are one amazing man.

To my family, you are a continual source of inspiration. Thank you for your unconditional love and support.

To my sister, Karen, you continually amaze me. Thank you for always being there. You are one of the most caring, compassionate and loving people I know. I am so proud to call you my sister and my best friend.

To my sweet momma and my biggest fan, I love you with all my heart.

To Pat and Evie, where would I be without you? You are friendship without bounds. I will not forget your kindness, wisdom and unconditional love that you shower upon me without measure.

To Jean and Sharon, thank you for your willingness to offer editorial support. Your friendship and love over the years has meant so much to me.

To Julie, Lisa and Lois, thank you for believing in this project and for believing in me and for all the ways that you have shown support. You went above and beyond my expectations time and time again.

To Steve, thank you for your support and technical expertise over the years. More than that, I thank you for your friendship and kindness.

To my board members past and present a heartfelt thanks.

I thank the people within Christian fundamentalism who parted ways with me because of our differing beliefs. Our shared experiences were difficult to say the least but without them I would not have written this book. You will always hold a place in my heart.

About the Author

Barbara Symons is an ordained minister and tireless spiritual seeker whose experience in Christian fundamentalism spans her lifetime beginning at five years of age. After leaving the church in 1999, Barbara began to recognize the fear-based propaganda that most fundamentalism employs. Having spent forty-three years within Christian fundamentalism, ten of those years as an exorcist, Barbara has keen insight into this systematic religion and writes of her journey through deprogramming. Always captivated by unusual phenomena, Barbara has a vast repertoire of spiritual and metaphysical experiences from which to draw. She is a lecturer, teacher and writer who hopes to bring light to the mysteries that can be found within the historical stories of the Bible and beyond.

Barbara resides in College Station, Texas and is married to Lyle. Together they have three children and five grandchildren.

Website: www.BarbaraSymons.com

Printed in Great Britain
by Amazon

32516807R00131